Be
Sri Lanka

Text by Gavin Thomas
Photography by Marcus Wilson-Smith and
David Henley
Series Editor: Tony Halliday

Berlitz® POCKET GUIDE

Sri Lanka

First Edition 2006

PHOTOGRAPHY
David Henley/Apa 6, 9, 29, 31, 34, 37, 40, 43, 44, 47, 49, 52, 59, 60, 65, 69, 80, 81, 84, 88, 93, 96, 99, 100, 105, 106; Getty Images 32; Imagebank/Getty Images 62–3; Marcus Wilson-Smith/Apa 10, 13, 14, 16, 24, 25, 30, 33, 35, 36, 39, 42, 51, 55, 56, 57, 64, 67, 69, 72, 74, 76, 79, 83, 86, 87, 89, 90, 102; Mary Evans 17, 18; Popperfoto/Alamy 20; Ravindralal Anthonis 70; TopFoto/ImageWorks 22
Cover photograph: U. and H. Kolley/Superstock

CONTACTING THE EDITORS
Every effort has been made to provide accurate information in this publication, but changes are inevitable. The publisher cannot be responsible for any resulting loss, inconvenience or injury. We would appreciate it if readers would call our attention to any errors or outdated information by contacting Berlitz Publishing, PO Box 7910, London SE1 1WE, England. Fax: (44) 20 7403 0290; e-mail: berlitz@apaguide.co.uk www.berlitzpublishing.com

> ➤
Minneriya and Kaudulla national parks (page 70) are famous for their extensive elephant populations

The perfectly preserved Dutch fort at Galle (page 35), is filled with atmospheric colonial buildings
▲

Explore the monasteries, shrines and colossal Buddhas of Polonnaruwa (page 65) ▼

TOP TEN ATTRACTIONS

Ahangama (page 37), one of the best places to see Sri Lanka's famous stilt-fishermen ▼

Kandy, home to the famous Temple of the Tooth, is a vibrant centre of Sinhalese culture (page 44) ◀

Nuwara Eliya, picturesque hill town from the colonial days and centre of Sri Lanka's tea cultivation (page 53) ▶

The west coast's premier beach destination, Bentota (page 32) has wide golden sands and stylish hotels ▼

Sigiriya (page 63) is a fascinating ancient citadel, featuring the so-called 'Sigiriya Damsels' ▶

See dawn's shadow cast from revered Adam's Peak (page 57) ▶

Anuradhapura (page 72), is home to an astonishing collection of stupas ▶

CONTENTS

Fact Sheets

INTRODUCTION

Poised a few degrees above the equator amidst the azure waters of the Indian Ocean, Sri Lanka is, for many visitors, one of Asia's ultimate tropical island paradises. Medieval traders and contemporary tourists alike have been beguiled by the island's endless miles of golden beaches and abundant natural riches, from cinnamon to sapphires and elephants. Marco Polo declared it the finest island of its size in the world, while generations of other travellers, from Ibn Battuta to Mark Twain, have waxed lyrical over the country's natural beauty and palm-fringed shores.

The tropical island stereotypes are only part of the truth, however. Although a relatively small nation by Asian standards, Sri Lanka has tremendous physical, cultural and ethnic diversity, as well as a long and distinguished history stretching far back into the pre-Christian era. As the home of one of the world's oldest and purest Buddhist traditions, Sri Lanka boasts a unique and distinctive cultural character, though one which has also been greatly enriched by long centuries of foreign influence. The island's wide range of landscapes, from tropical beaches to misty upland tea plantations, lends it an extraordinary scenic appeal.

The Modern Nation

The Democratic Socialist Republic of Sri Lanka (as it has been known since 1972, when it ditched the old British colonial name of Ceylon) now boasts a population approaching 20 million, and is growing rapidly. Almost three-quarters of the population are Buddhist Sinhalese, the descendants of settlers from North India, but there are also

Tangalla coastline

significant numbers of South Indian-descended Hindu Tamils, particularly in the north and east of the island. The nation's two main languages are Sinhala (the language of the Sinhalese) and Tamil, while English is also widely spoken. The island has been a multi-party democracy since independence in 1948.

Sri Lanka's recent history has been overshadowed by the civil war between the Sri Lankan government and the separatist Tamil Tigers (LTTE), which ravaged the island throughout the 1980s and 1990s. A ceasefire was finally negotiated in 2001, and though the peace has so far held, Sinhalese-Tamil

The Many Names of Sri Lanka

Sri Lanka has had many names over the centuries. The island's ancient Sanskrit name was Sinhaladvipa, 'Lion Island', named after the Sinhalese themselves, and it was this name which provided the basis for most of the island's subsequent monikers. In Pali, the classic language of early Buddhism, Sinhala is 'Sihalam', pronounced 'Silam', which was subsequently bastardised by the Portuguese into Ceilão, by the Dutch to Zeylan, and by the British to Ceylon. Early Arab traders, meanwhile, transformed it into Serendib, the origin of the English word 'serendipity', signifying the making of happy discoveries by chance, a word which is still much used to describe Sri Lanka's fortuitous pleasures.

Not that these were the island's only names. The island was also known in ancient Sanskrit literature as Ratnadvipa ('Island of Gems'), while the Greeks and Romans knew it as Taprobane, a mutation of another ancient Sanskrit name for the island, Tambapanni ('copper-coloured'), derived from the colour of the beach on which Prince Vijaya first landed. For the Sinhalese, however, the island has always been Lanka – as it is called in the great Indian epic the *Ramayana* – and it was to this name, with the additional 'Sri', meaning 'resplendent' or 'auspicious', that the nation's name officially reverted in 1972.

tensions continue to rumble ominously beneath the surface of national life. Tragically, having finally emerged from two decades of civil war, the island's prospects were further blighted by the 2004 Asian tsunami, which killed almost 40,000 people on Sri Lanka alone and reduced much of the seaboard to ruins. However, subsequent reconstruction of coastal tourist areas has been swift and thorough, and the island's tourist facilities are

Waterfall in the hill country

now of a higher standard than ever before, reflecting the industry's increasingly crucial role in the national economy.

Landscapes

One of Sri Lanka's greatest attractions is the remarkable range of landscapes that are packed into the island's modest dimensions. It is possible to wake up sweating on the coast and then be shivering by lunchtime in the breezy heights of the hill country, just a few hours' drive away. Most of the island's 1,340km (830 miles) of coastline is fringed with idyllic golden-sand beaches, many of which remain remarkably undeveloped, offering a perfect tropical bolthole for those wishing to escape the commercialisation that has overtaken many other parts of Asia.

Away from the sultry coast lies a world of scenic contrasts, from the rugged mountains and misty green uplands of the hill country to the rolling, wildlife-rich savannahs of the north and east. Thorny dry monsoon forest carpets much of the lowland plains, while tea plantations blanket the hills, dotted with perfectly preserved pockets of rainforest and cloudforest. This physical variety in turn supports a uniquely varied array of flora and fauna, including thousands of wild elephants, one of the world's largest leopard populations, and a vast number of bird species, many of which are found only on the island.

One Island, Many People

The island's physical diversity is mirrored by its cosmopolitan cultural make-up, the legacy of centuries of commerce and conquest experienced by Sri Lanka thanks to its strategic position on the trade routes of the Indian Ocean. Foremost amongst the island's myriad ethnic groups are the Sinhalese, originally from North India, who arrived in Sri Lanka sometime around the 4th or 5th century BC. The Sinhalese now make up over two-thirds of the population and have given the country its rich Buddhist traditions and a religious outlook that continues to shape the nation.

Tamils from South India, who have probably been in Sri Lanka as long as the Sinhalese, make up the island's second-largest ethnic group and have created a vibrant local Hindu culture which runs parallel to the Buddhist majority. Waves of Arab, Indian and Malay traders and

Boy monks at Sigiriya

Portuguese, Dutch and British settlers have also left their mark on everything from the island's cooking and architecture to its religion, railways and economy.

Some sense of Sri Lanka's cultural diversity can be gleaned by comparing the contrasting lifestyles of two of its smallest but most distinctive ethnic groups. In Colombo, the urbane Burghers – white, English-speaking Sri Lankans of mixed European descent – still play a leading role in the island's cultural life. In the remote jungles of the east, a handful of aboriginal Veddahs, the island's oldest inhabitants, who have lived here for at least 18,000 years, continue to pursue their traditional hunter-gatherer existence.

Buddhas and Beaches

The Sinhalese civilisation can be traced back to the 3rd century BC, when Buddhism first arrived on here. By the 1st century AD the great city of Anuradhapura had developed into a vibrant centre of Buddhist learning, its sizeable population of monks supported by the immense irrigation works with which the early Sinhalese transformed the island's arid northern plains into a fertile rice bowl. The remains of this early Sinhalese civilisation, found at Anuradhapura, Sigiriya and Polonnaruwa, include an astonishing array of monasteries, shrines, statues and vast stupas, the largest man-made structures in the ancient world, bar the two largest Egyptian pyramids.

Sri Lanka's other attractions are legion, from the atmospheric tea plantations of the hill country to the vibrant cultural traditions of Kandy and the more contemporary urban attractions of Colombo. It is now also possible to strike off into the north or east of the island, only recently reopened to casual visitors after the years of civil war (with the recent upsurge in violence it's wise to check the situation on the ground before deciding whether to travel to these areas). If none of the above appeal, you can always simply go and lie on a beach.

A BRIEF HISTORY

Sri Lanka's abundant natural resources and its pivotal location at a major crossroads of the Indian Ocean's trading routes have attracted myriad different adventurers, traders and settlers over the centuries. It has been laid open to an enormous variety of influences which can still be seen in everything from the island's religions and culture to its architecture and cuisine.

Prehistory

Early archaeological evidence of human settlement in Sri Lanka remains slight. The first people to arrive on the island were the Veddahs, an aboriginal hunter-gatherer people thought to be related to the aboriginal peoples of Australia, Malaysia and the Nicobar Islands. They are believed to have arrived in Sri Lanka by around 16,000BC, or possibly much earlier, and survive in isolated pockets in the east of the island in ever-diminishing numbers.

Starting around the 5th century BC, waves of settlers began to arrive in Sri Lanka from northern India. The first arrivals are thought to have come from modern Gujarat, and were followed by further immigrants from Orissa and Bengal. These people, the ancestors of the modern Sinhalese, initially settled on the west coast and gradually pushed inland towards the centre of the northern plains where, in around 377BC, they established the settlement of Anuradhapura. This was Sri Lanka's first great city and remained the focus of the island's history for almost 1,500 years.

The Anuradhapura Period

The first major landmark in the development of Anuradhapura was the arrival of Buddhism in 246BC, brought to the island by Mahinda, the son of the great Indian Buddhist emperor Asoka. Mahinda quickly converted the Sinhalese king, Devanampiya Tissa, who embraced the new faith enthusiastically. Buddhism provided the Sinhalese with an important sense of national identity, and Anuradhapura soon developed a markedly religious emphasis with the establishment of the great Mahavihara monastery and other Buddhist institutions.

Ruvanvalisaya stupa at Anuradhapura

Soon after Devanampiya Tissa's death, however, Anuradhapura suffered the first of the invasions by Tamils from south India which were to prove a recurrent feature of its entire history. The Tamil general Elara ruled for 44 years before the famous warrior-king Dutugemunu succeeded in ousting the Tamils, uniting the entire island under Sinhalese rule for the first time.

The subsequent history of Anuradhapura repeated the theme thus established, with periods of relative stability interspersed with chaotic intervals during which Tamil invaders and Sinhalese infighting threw the island into disarray. In AD473, for example, the notorious Kassapa murdered his father, King Dhatusena, and briefly established a rival capital at Sigiriya. Despite these periodic upheavals, Anuradhapura developed into one of the great cities of its age. Huge tracts of the arid surrounding plains were irrigated and vast reservoirs were built *(see page 74)*, while the city's great monasteries served as bastions of the Buddhist faith and learning. During the 9th and 10th centuries, however, repeated Tamil invasions slowly brought Anuradhapura to its knees, until in 993 the army of the Chola king Rajaraja sacked the city, an event from which it never recovered.

Polonnaruwa Period

Having reduced Anuradhapura to rubble, the Cholas established a new capital at the city of Polonnaruwa. The site had the great strategic advantage of being further from India, and thus less vulnerable to foreign interference, and the Cholas ruled there for 75 years until they were toppled by another great Sinhalese warrior-king, Vijayabahu. Vijayabahu's reconquest of Polonnaruwa ushered in a final golden age of

Gal Vilhara at Polonnaruwa – a golden age of Sinhalese culture

Sinhalese culture in the north. His successor, Parakram-abahu, transformed the city into one of the finest of its age, and a rival to the abandoned Anuradhapura. Once again, however, Tamil invaders were to prove the Sinhalese capital's undoing. In 1212 a new wave of Pandyan invaders arrived, and in 1215 the infamous Magha seized control of Polonnaruwa. His chaotic reign of terror left the city crippled, the monasteries shattered and the great irrigation systems of the north in chronic disrepair, signalling the end of the great early Sinhalese civilisations of northern Sri Lanka.

Sinhalese Decline and the Rise of Jaffna

As Polonnaruwa crumbled, so the Sinhalese nobility gradually migrated south towards the relative safety of the hill country, establishing a series of transient capitals whose kings enjoyed increasingly limited control over the island as a whole. Over the next two centuries the island's great Buddhist institutions collapsed, whilst Tamil Hindu influence began to permeate the island's culture and religion. At the same time, yet another wave of Tamil invaders established a vibrant new kingdom centred on the city of Jaffna, at the northernmost point of the island, from where they gradually pushed south and east, establishing the Tamil–Sinhalese cultural divide which endures to this day.

The Portuguese

By the beginning of the 16th century, the remnants of the Sinhalese aristocracy had established two major rival centres of power: one in the hills at Kandy, and another near the coast at Kotte, near present-day Colombo. It was the Kingdom of Kotte which was the first to experience the depredations of a new and more exotic wave of invaders, the Portuguese. The Portuguese arrived in 1505 in search of spices, and soon established a fort at Colombo (the origin of

**Entrance to Dutch-built Fort
Frederick, Trincomalee**

the modern city), from where they engaged in periodic skirmishes with Kotte. Although the Sinhalese were initially able to resist Portuguese attacks on land, they had no response to the Europeans' sea power. The Portuguese gradually spread out along the coast, annexing the declining Kingdom of Jaffna in 1619 and fighting their way around the seaboard until they had established control over much of the island's lowlands, taking over the Sinhalese king's monopoly on the sale of elephants, as well as the lucrative trade in spices such as pepper and betel nut. The Portuguese invasion was accompanied by a fervent campaign of missionary activity, with considerable swathes of the coastal population converted to Catholicism and numerous temples destroyed. This explains the origin of the numerous Sri Lankan de Silvas, Pereiras and Fernandos whose names fill the island's telephone directories to this day.

The Kandyan Kingdom and the Dutch

One final bastion of Sinhalese power remained, however: the Kingdom of Kandy, buried deep in the impenetrable hills of the interior. The Portuguese were unable to subdue Kandy, despite repeated attempts – while the Kandyans, in turn, launched offensives against the Portuguese, though their lack of sea power prevented them from permanently evicting the European interlopers. It was the hope of driving the Portuguese out of Sri Lanka once and for all that led the

Kandyans into an unlikely alliance with another European power, the Dutch, who had increasingly begun to covet the island's rich natural resources.

Between 1638 and 1658 the Dutch systematically attacked and overran Portuguese coastal strongholds, though they showed no signs of handing any of these conquered territories back to the Kandyans. Having established their mastery over much of the island, the pragmatic Dutch set about promoting trade and systematically exploiting the island's commercial possibilities. They also made modest efforts to promote their Calvinist Protestant faith at the expense of Catholicism, which they declared illegal.

The British

A Dutch settlement, 1682

It was, however, the third and final of the colonial powers to occupy Sri Lanka, the British, who were to exercise the most lasting influence on the island. Like the Dutch, the British (already firmly established in neighbouring India) had had their eyes on Sri Lanka – particularly the strategic deep-water harbour at Trincomalee – for some years. Unlike the Dutch, they were able to take possession of the island with a minimum of military fuss thanks to the Napoleonic Wars in Europe. When the Netherlands fell to the French in 1794, the British stepped in to 'protect' the Dutch colony from French interference. The Dutch mounted only token resistance, and British possession of the island was formally ratified by the Treaty of Amiens in 1802.

Like the Dutch, British policy in Sri Lanka was largely aimed at maximising the island's commercial potential and their legacies – most notably the country's tea industry, its railways, and the English language itself – remain essential elements of the modern island's commercial and cultural landscape. The British also finally succeeded in taking possession of the recalcitrant Kandyan Kingdom, thanks to the efforts of the arch colonial schemer Sir John D'Oyly, who succeeded in turning the kingdom's Sinhalese nobles against their Tamil king. In 1815, after three centuries of spirited and often bloody resistance, the Kandyans meekly surrendered, finally extinguishing the last bastion of independent native rule in the island.

A European in a rickshaw, 1933

Towards Independence

The later part of the 19th century was a period of intense soul-searching for the Sinhalese. Faced with an occupying and unshiftable European power and the constantly encroaching influence of missionary Christianity, the islanders began to re-evaluate their traditional religious and cultural beliefs, creating a vigorous Buddhist revivalist movement. As the 20th century dawned, this movement became increasingly politicised, leading to the foundation of the Ceylon National Congress in 1919. The British gradually began to make concessions, and in 1931 a new constitution gave the island's political leaders the first opportunity to exercise real (though still limited) political power, as well as granting the islanders universal suffrage.

During World War II Sri Lanka became a strategically vital base for British operations in Asia following the fall of Indonesia, Burma and Singapore to the Japanese. It even attracted the attentions of the Japanese air force, who launched raids against Colombo and Trincomalee. Following the war, the enfeebled British Empire gave up its colonial possessions, and Sri Lanka finally achieved independence on 6 February, 1948.

Independence

Power was handed to the United National Party (UNP), a generally conservative party dominated by the English-educated leaders such as the Senanayake family, who had risen to prominence under the British. The UNP ruled until 1956, when they were ousted by the more populist and nationalist Sri Lanka Freedom Party (SLFP), led by the charismatic S.W.R.D. Bandaranaike. These two parties have alternated in power ever since – with the Senanayake and Bandaranaike families (or their close relatives) providing most of the island's leaders right up to the present day. This

S.W.R.D. Bandaranaike

has particularly been the case with the SLFP. When S.W.R.D. Bandaranaike was assassinated by a Buddhist monk in 1959, leadership of the party passed quickly to his widow, Srimavo, who thus became the world's first ever female prime minister. Their daughter, Chandrika Kumaratunga would later serve as both prime minister and president, a dynastic family sequence to rival the Nehrus in India, and one which gained the SLFP the nickname of the 'Sri Lanka Family Party'.

The early years of Independence were kind to Sri Lanka, but during the 1950s and 1960s increasing economic difficulties and falling living standards led to widespread disenchantment, culminating in the 1971 armed rebellion staged by the JVP, a quasi-Marxist, student-led organisation with a pronounced nationalistic, anti-Tamil stance. The insurrection was put down with considerable loss of life, but anti-Tamil rhetoric became a feature of national political life. A controversial sequence of legislative changes drove the Tamils into the margins of the island's commercial and political life. A new generation of militant Tamil organisations sprang up in the north of the island – including the Tamil Tigers, or LTTE – and the number of confrontations between them and the Sri Lankan police and army began to increase.

Civil War

Anti-Tamil sentiment reached a peak in 1983 when, following an LTTE massacre of an army patrol in the north, Sinhalese mobs launched an orgy of violence against Tamils across the island, killing as many as 2,000 people. Thousands of Tamils fled to the north or departed overseas, while corresponding numbers of Sinhalese came south. By 1985 the conflict had developed into an all-out civil war between the Sinhalese-dominated Sri Lankan Army (SLA) and the guerrilla forces of the LTTE.

In 1987 the Indian government, under increasing pressure from its own enormous Tamil population, intervened in the conflict by despatching the hugely controversial Indian Peace-Keeping Force (IPKF) to the island to enforce a ceasefire. It rapidly became embroiled in heavy fighting with the Tamils it had allegedly come to protect. Meanwhile, in 1987, a second JVP rebellion broke out in the south, reducing the entire island to a state of near anarchy.

The JVP rebellion was once again put down with brutal force, while in 1990 the IPKF, facing mounting casualties, left the island, to the relief of both Tamils and Sinhalese. The remainder of the decade was the most dismal in modern Sri Lankan history. Heavy fighting continued throughout the north and east between the LTTE and SLA, while repeated LTTE suicide-bomber attacks against Colombo and other southern targets claimed thousands of civilian casualties. As the conflict dragged on, it became increasingly obvious that neither side could hope for outright victory, and by the end of the century there was still no sign that the conflict which had already claimed an estimated 60,000 lives would end.

The end of civil war arrived suddenly, however. In 2001 the LTTE announced a ceasefire, which was declared permanent in February 2002. Later in the year they made one of their most important concessions, by abandoning their demand for complete independence in favour of a federal system whereby they agreed to Sri Lanka remaining a single nation.

Following the ceasefire, a wave of optimism swept the country. The economy and tourist industries boomed, while Jaffna and Trincomalee reopened to visitors for the first time in almost 20 years. But negotiations soon ran into difficulties amidst mounting suspicion on both sides. By the end of 2004 the peace process had ground to a halt.

The Tsunami

On 26 December 2004, the island suffered a natural catastrophe whose devastating effects dwarfed even the two decades of civil war. A massive tsunami caused by an underwater earthquake off the coast of Sumatra inundated around three-quarters of the island's densely populated coastline, killing some 38,000 people and reducing many settlements around the coast to rubble. Despite an overwhelming international response to the disaster, the government has been slow to release aid to many affected villages. Arguments about the distribution of aid to the north and east have further deepened Tamil-Sinhalese divisions – an additional blow to the seemingly permanently stalled peace process.

Tsunami devastation in Galle

Historical Landmarks

c. **16,000**BC Arrival of Veddahs.

c. **500**BC Arrival of first Sinhalese settlers.

377BC Foundation of Anuradhapura.

247BC King Devanampiya Tissa converts to Buddhism.

161BC Dutugemunu establishes first island-wide Sinhalese kingdom.

AD473 Kassapa establishes short-lived capital at Sigiriya.

993 Cholas establish new capital at Polonnaruwa.

1070 Vijayabahu drives out Cholas and re-establishes Sinhalese rule.

1215 Tamil mercenary Magha seizes control of Polonnaruwa.

13th–15th centuries Series of short-lived Sinhalese capitals, leading to establishment of Kandy and Kotte. Rise of Jaffna kingdom.

1505 Arrival of Portuguese, and establishment of fort in Colombo.

1619 Portuguese annexe Jaffna.

1638 Beginning of Dutch attacks against Portuguese.

1658 Jaffna falls to Dutch; end of Portuguese power in Sri Lanka.

1796 British take control of Sri Lanka from Dutch.

1867 First tea plantation established. Colombo to Kandy railway built.

1919 Foundation of Ceylon National Congress, first nationalist party.

1948 Country achieves independence. Changes name to Sri Lanka.

1959 Prime minister S.W.R.D. Dandaranaike assassinated by a Buddhist monk. His widow becomes the world's first female prime minister.

1971 Armed insurrection against government by JVP.

1972 Country becomes Democratic Socialist Republic of Sri Lanka.

1983 Civil war erupts between government forces and LTTE, following island-wide massacres of Tamils by Sinhalese mobs.

1987 Arrival of Indian Peace-Keeping Force (IPKF) in the north.

1990 Departure of IPKF after failure to keep the peace.

1993 Suicide bomber kills prime minister Ranasinghe Premadasa.

1996 Sri Lanka co-hosts and wins World Cricket Cup.

2001 LTTE declares ceasefire, ending two decades of civil war.

2004 Tsunami devastates coastal areas of island, killing thousands.

2006 Ceasefire undermined by an upsurge in violence.

WHERE TO GO

A classic Sri Lankan itinerary would include a few days in the Cultural Triangle, a tour through Kandy and the hill country, and a spell spent on the beaches of the southern or western coast. These places offer an overview of the island's contrasting landscapes and complex history, but they are by no means all the country has to offer. Hiring a car and driver *(see page 122)* means you get to see a lot more than you otherwise would, but you still won't get anywhere fast. You will, however, get a feeling for the island's essentially rural lifestyle and sleepy pace of life.

COLOMBO

In a predominantly rural island, Colombo is Sri Lanka's one true metropolis. Home to around three million people and most of the island's significant commercial and industrial activity, the city sprawls along the west coast for the best part of 60km (40 miles), an endless straggle of chaotic and traffic-infested suburbs which can seem totally out of scale and character with the rest of the island. Unsurprisingly, this noisy, crowded and disorienting urban morass ranks low on most tourist itineraries, but despite initial impressions, there is plenty in the city's contrasting districts and a handful of low-key sights to merit at least a day's exploration.

Fort and the Pettah

The heart of old Colombo is **Fort** district, first established by the Portuguese, who constructed the now vanished fortifications after which the district is named. Once the centrepiece of Colombo's commercial and administrative life, Fort bore

Gangaramaya Temple, Colombo

Galle Face Green

the brunt of repeated LTTE attacks against Colombo during the civil war, and is now rather forlorn, with a heavy army presence and large areas closed off for security reasons. The heart of the district is marked by a quaint **clocktower-cum-lighthouse**, erected in 1857, while other crumbling relics of 19th-century British enterprise lie dotted around, most notably the famous old **Cargills** department store. At the southern edge of the district rises an incongruous cluster of high-rises containing several five-star hotels and the twin towers of the **World Trade Centre**.

East of Fort lies Colombo's most absorbing area, **The Pettah**, a crowded and chaotic bazaar district whose tight grid of streets is crammed full of an astonishing number of shops whose owners frantically trade everything from Ayurvedic herbs to mobile phones. At the heart of the district, the **Dutch Period Museum** (open Tues–Sat 9am–5pm; admission fee) houses a modest selection of exhibits relating to

Dutch life in colonial Sri Lanka in an atmospheric old villa. Just to the north is the **Jami al-Aftar** mosque, the district's most eye-catching landmark, its exterior decorated in bright red and white stripes.

Galle Face Green and Slave Island

South of Fort stretches **Galle Face Green**, bounded to the north by the high-rises of Fort and the sprawling neoclassical Government Secretariat, and to the south by the famous old colonial **Galle Face Hotel**. A favourite city meeting place, the green really comes alive towards dusk when half the city descends on it to swap gossip, fly kites, enjoy the sea breezes and sample the unusual snacks served up by innumerable stalls set up along the promenade.

Heading inland from Galle Face Green, the ramshackle district of **Slave Island** (named after the African slaves once corralled here by the Portuguese and Dutch) is home to a cluster of Hindu and Buddhist shrines, including the city's two most interesting Buddhist temples. The first is the unusual **Seema Malaka** (designed by Sri Lanka's foremost 20th-century architect, Geoffrey Bawa), whose wooden buildings occupy three platforms set out over the waters of Lake Beira – particularly beautiful when illuminated at night. Just east of here, the more extensive and traditional **Gangaramaya** comprises a peaceful little courtyard surrounded by shrines populated by assorted deities, including a huge modern ceramic Buddha. The quirky attached museum (admission fee) displays thousands of gifts presented to the temple over the years, including an unusual selection of vintage cars.

The Dutch discouraged slaves from attempting to escape Slave Island by keeping a healthy population of crocodiles in the surrounding canals and the waters of Beira Lake.

Southern Colombo

South of Slave Island, the serene suburb of **Cinnamon Gardens** is the city's smartest address, with leafy roads lined with grand colonial villas and the peaceful **Viharamahadevi Park**, which stretches south of the modern town hall. The park is home to the **National Museum** (open daily except Fri 9am–5pm; admission fee). Occupying one of Colombo's finest colonial buildings, the museum's extensive collection includes some fine ancient Buddhist and Hindu statuary, an excellent selection of *kolam* masks and the lavish regalia of the last king of Kandy. South of Galle Face Green, southern Colombo's major traffic artery, the smelly and congested Galle Road, strikes due south through the districts of Kollupitiya and Bambalapitiya, now home to many of the city's top shops and restaurants, including the outstanding Barefoot shop and the beautiful Gallery Café *(see pages 86–7 and 138–9)*. A few kilometres further south, **Dehiwala Zoo** (open daily 8.30am–6pm; admission fee) is home to a comprehensive collection of international and indigenous wildlife, including a good selection of the island's local fauna, from sloth bears to leopards.

At the southern edge of Colombo, 10km (6 miles) south of Fort, the laid-back suburb of **Mount Lavinia** offers a peaceful respite from the city streets to the north, presided over by the venerable **Mount Lavinia Hotel**, whose graceful white buildings provide the suburb's major landmark. Although it is more popular with locals than with foreign tourists, the stretch of rather grubby beach here – the closest to the city centre – makes it a popular spot, particularly at weekends.

Ten kilometres east of Fort lies the **Kelaniya Raja Maha Vihara**, the most important Buddhist shrine in Colombo. Built to commemorate the third and last of the Buddha's visits to the island, the modern temple complex comprises a vibrant and colourful array of modern paintings and sculptures, and is always lively with pilgrims.

THE WEST COAST

Sri Lanka's west coast is the most developed part of the island, and its innumerable large-scale resort hotels remain the driving force behind the country's sizeable package-tourist industry. Much of the development here has been extensive and unregulated, and if you want unspoiled beaches and a true taste of the island's fabled serenity you will have to head further south. Having said that, the west coast is home to many of Sri Lanka's finest beachside hotels, both large and small, and still offers pockets of tropical charm, if you know where to look.

Negombo and Around

Thirty kilometres (20 miles) north of Colombo, **Negombo** owes its popularity mainly to its proximity to the international airport, offering a convenient first (or last) stop on a tour of the

Mending nets at Negombo

island. The wide beach here has a plethora of guesthouses and resort hotels, and although there are far nicer beaches further south, Negombo has enough tropical charm to merit a day's rest and recuperation after a long-haul flight. Tourists share the beach with the local Karava fishermen, whose flotillas of oruwa boats make a memorable sight as they return from off-shore fishing trips during the early morning. Ingeniously constructed, an *oruwa* is fashioned from narrow canoes topped by an enormous sail which is kept steady in the water by cantilevered wooden floats. This type of vessel is known in Tamil as *ketti-maran*, the origin of the word 'catamaran'.

South of the resort, **Negombo town** is dominated by the enormous pink bulk of **St Mary's Church**, testament to the town's status as one of the strongholds of Christianity on the west coast. The town was formerly an important Dutch settlement thanks to its strategic control of the lucrative local cinna-

Oruwas returning to harbour

mon trade and it preserves a few traces of its colonial heritage, including fragments of an old **Dutch fort**, as well as its old **Dutch canal**, which runs due north along the coast all the way to Puttalam, some 80km (50 miles) distant. It is possible to organise **boat trips** along the canal or off the coast in oruwa boats as well as through the wetlands of **Muthurajawela**, south of the town, home to rich bird life and other fauna.

Negombo fish market

Kalutara

Just south of the great urban sprawl of Colombo, **Kalutara** has a long stretch of fine, though rather narrow, beach backed by a string of large-scale resort hotels. The lively town itself is worth a visit for the **Gangatilaka Vihara**, a picturesque temple whose enormous stupa looms imposingly over the main coastal road. The stupa also has the unusual distinction of being the only entirely hollow one in the world – step inside to experience the resonant echoes and murals depicting scenes from the Buddha's life.

Beruwala, Bentota and Around

The epicentre of the Sri Lankan package-tourist industry lies further south at the twin resorts of Beruwala and Bentota. **Beruwala** is the most developed resort in the island, with a beautiful wide stretch of fine golden sand flanked by a dense concentration of hotels mainly catering for European sun seekers during the northern winter. South of here,

Bentota has an equally fine swathe of sand, but the atmosphere is more laid-back. With a sequence of fine hotels strung at discreet intervals along the coast, this is the most pleasant beach destination along the west coast. Bentota is also the island's water sports capital, with numerous activities ranging from jet-skiing to windsurfing on the tranquil waters of the **Bentota lagoon**, which meanders inland from here, and also offers a rewarding destination for boat trips into its tangled waterways and mangrove swamps. Both Beruwala and Bentota have a selection of diving schools, as well as the densest concentration of ayurvedic hotels on the island.

A few turtle hatcheries also dot the coast, most notably the **Sea Turtles Project** (open daily 8am–6pm; admission fee) at the southern end of Bentota. Here you can see tanks full of minuscule baby turtles, which are held here for a few

Palm-fringed Bentota beach

days before being released back into the ocean.

Sandwiched between Bentota and Beruwala, the little workaday town of **Aluthgama** is home to a cluster of attractive low-key guesthouses backing the Bentota lagoon, and offers a refreshing slice of everyday Sri Lankan life amidst the tourist development, with colourful fish and vegetable

Brief Gardens

markets. A few kilometres inland lies the picture-perfect little estate of **Brief Gardens** (open daily 8am–5pm; admission fee) which was established by the famous Sri Lankan socialite, amateur artist and man-of-letters Bewis Bawa. His father was a lawyer who bought the estate with the fee won from a successfully contested legal brief – hence the name. Bewis's work in transforming Brief Gardens inspired his brother, the great architect Geoffrey Bawa (himself a failed lawyer) to turn his hand to designing buildings. The estate comprises a small but exquisite garden surrounding an artfully restored colonial villa stuffed full of artworks, photographs and other intriguing mementos.

Ambalangoda

About 25km (15 miles) south of Bentota, the small town of **Ambalangoda** has another fine swathe of sand, though it is best known as the centre of the Sri Lankan mask-making industry, whose grotesque faces, representing various demons and humans, leer at you from shops and houses all over the south of the island. A copious selection of masks, and descriptions of the dances they were originally designed for, can be

Sri Lanka's most popular mask is Gurulu Raksha, a terrifying bird-like creature who is believed to prey on snakes and demons. Many people in the south hang Gurulu Raksha masks outside their houses to ward off malign influences.

seen in the **Ariyapala and Sons Mask Museum** (open daily 8.30am–5.30pm; donation requested). This rewarding museum has a large shop selling the most extensive selection of masks anywhere on the island – you can also see them being made in the attached workshop. If you want to see the masks used in the dances for which they were originally intended, you may be able to watch rehearsals and performances by students at the nearby **Bandu Wijesurya School of Dance** – ask at the museum for details.

Hikkaduwa

Close to the southernmost point of the west coast, **Hikkaduwa** offers a down-at-heel alternative to the big resorts further north. Back in the 1970s, Hikkaduwa was Sri Lanka's original hippy hangout, and although uncontrolled development here has taken a massive toll on the beach and town, the resort remains modestly popular amongst backpackers, surfers and divers, and has a liveliness lacking in the sedate resorts further up the coast. The famous **coral sanctuary**, a once-beautiful section of reef in shallow water just off the beach in the centre of town, is worth a visit. Although the coral is now largely dead, you can still see tropical fish. Hikkaduwa also offers some of the best surfing in Sri Lanka, as well as the island's best selection of diving schools.

THE SOUTH

In many ways, the south is Sri Lanka at its most quintessentially Sri Lankan, with thousands of comatose villages, nestled under great swathes of palm trees, where the pace of life still travels at the speed of the bicycle rather than the car, and where coconuts are considered more important than computers. For visitors, the region offers a beguiling mixture of culture and hedonism. A long sequence of beautiful and largely unspoilt beaches is interspersed with national parks and some important Buddhist shrines – physical evidence of the south's traditional role as a bastion of Sinhalese Buddhist culture.

Galle

The gateway to the south is the beautiful old settlement of **Galle** (pronounced 'Gaul'), Sri Lanka's best-preserved colonial city. First established by the Portuguese, the old part of the city, known as **Galle Fort**, achieved its present shape largely thanks to the Dutch, who erected a great chain of walls and bastions to protect the settlement from invaders. The streets inside are filled with atmospheric villas hidden behind enormous, shady verandahs and topped with crumbling red-tiled roofs – a wonderful place for an aimless and pleasantly traffic-free stroll.

Galle lighthouse and ramparts

Galle's Historical Mansion Museum

Entrance to the town is through the **Main Gate**, a narrow portal cut into the enormous bastions, facing the cricket ground and modern city. From here, Church Street veers round to the left, taking you past several of Galle's main sights, including the rather dull little **National Museum, Galle** (open Tues–Sat 9am–5pm; admission fee) and the ultra-deluxe Amman Hotel, occupying a building originally built for the Dutch governor in 1684. Just past here is the intriguing **Dutch Reformed Church** of 1755: elegantly Italianate on the outside; severely plain within, apart from the many elaborately carved memorials to the city's Dutch and British settlers.

Continue south to the junction with Queen's Street, marked by a further clutch of colonial buildings, including **All Saint's Church**, whose chunky little spire provides an important city landmark, and the sprawling orange bulk of the **Great Warehouse**. Heading south along Leyn Baan Street brings you to the quirky **Historical Mansion Museum** (open daily 9am–6pm; donation requested), home to a vast collection of antiques and bric-a-brac assembled by its owner over the past 35 years. At the southern end of Leyn Baan Street is the florid **Meeran Jumma Mosque** and the **lighthouse**, from where it is possible to walk (clockwise) around the bastions all the way back to the Main Gate.

Unawatuna to Mirissa

Past Galle, the coast is dotted with a string of small villages, which survive on a mixture of fishing, coconut farming and low-level tourism. A few kilometres beyond Galle lies the personable little village of **Unawatuna**, which has long-since taken over from Hikkaduwa as Sri Lanka's most popular backpacker destination. A beautiful semi-circular beach is backed by a cluster of informal little guesthouses whose rickety wooden structures and string of beachfront cafés lend the place a genuine ad hoc charm. The atmosphere strikes the perfect balance between liveliness and somnolence.

Past Unawatuna, the coastal highway runs close to the sea, running through the small town of **Koggala**, home to the interesting **Martin Wickramasinghe Museum** (open daily 9am–5pm; admission fee), with an intriguing collection of local artefacts relating to the traditional Sinhalese way of life. Beyond Koggala, the town of **Ahangama** is one of the best places in Sri Lanka to see the famous **stilt fishermen**, who sit perched on poles amidst the waves casting their

Stilt fisherman of Ahangama

The enormous rocky outcrop backing Unawatuna village, Rumassala, is popularly believed to have been dropped by the monkey god Hanuman during his adventures in Sri Lanka described in the great Indian epic, the *Ramayana*.

lines in the waters. Immediately beyond Ahangama, the village of **Midigama** has a narrow beach, a handful of simple guesthouses and some of Sri Lanka's best surf.

The next town of any consequence along the coastal highway is **Weligama**, a sleepy little place whose quiet streets are lined with chintzy villas decorated with ornately carved wooden eaves. In front of the town, the wide sweep of Weligama Bay is dotted with a couple of tiny islets, most notably **Taprobane**, topped by a crown of tropical greenery and home to a luxury holiday villa. The beach here is long, wide and largely untouched, although most visitors now prefer to crash out at the tiny village of **Mirissa**, on the headland at the far end of the bay, where a small stretch of golden sand nestles beautifully behind a thick screen of palm trees. There is very little to do at either Weligama or Mirissa bar a bit of diving or snorkelling, but for many people that is the whole charm of being here.

Matara

A few kilometres beyond Mirissa, the bustling little city of **Matara** is the only settlement of any significant size in the south besides Galle, and is home to one of the country's leading universities. Like Galle, Matara rose to prominence under the Dutch, who fortified the town and made it an important settlement in the elephant and cinnamon trade. A line of coral-stone ramparts divides the modern city from the old colonial district, or **Fort**, which is bisected by peaceful streets of decaying old villas.

Much of the modern town lies on the north side of the palm-lined waters of the Nilwala Ganga river, and it is worth crossing over to visit the quaint little Dutch **Star Fort** of 1763, now home to a modest museum. A couple of kilometres outside town, the modern temple at **Weherehena** is home to one of the biggest Buddhas in the island, a 39-m (129-ft) gaudily painted colossus seated in deep meditation.

Tangalla and Around

There is another decent beach in the suburbs of Matara at **Polhena**, but most foreign tourists press on either west to Mirissa and Unawatuna, or further east to **Tangalla**, where more beaches dot the coast on either side of the scruffy little town. Although the beaches here are not as nice as others along the south coast, Tangalla has the bonus of a number of interesting sights in the surrounding countryside, which are

Fishing boats at Weligama

easily combined in a half-day's excursion. These include the unusual blowhole at **Hoo-maniya**, where a narrow cleft in the rock at the edge of the ocean sends enormous plumes of water up to 15m (50ft) high into the air; and the temple at **Wewurukannala**, whose impressive complex is home to another gigantic Buddha statue; at around 50m (160ft) high even bigger than the one at Weherehena.

Close to Tangalla is another major man-made attraction: the rock temples of **Mulkirigala**. Something of a cross between Dambulla and Sigiriya, the temples are carved into the flanks of a majestic rocky outcrop which rises dramatically out of the predominantly flat surrounding landscape. Seven hundred steps lead to the top of the rock, passing a sequence of temples arranged on four terraces carved out of the sides of the outcrop, which are filled with ornate Buddha statues and wall paintings dating back to the 18th century. At the top, the effort of the climb is rewarded by marvellous views south to the coast and north to the rolling uplands of the hill country.

The temple at Wewurukannala

Bundala National Park

Continuing east along the coast from Tangalla brings you to **Rekawa**, whose beach is one of the most important turtle-nesting sites in the islands. Locals here organise ad hoc nightly turtle watches (admission fee), during which it is possible to get a glimpse of these majestic creatures dragging themselves laboriously up onto the beach to bury their eggs in the sand.

Beyond Rekawa, the landscape changes as you enter the island's dry zone, the lush palm forests of the west and southwest coasts giving way to an arid, savannah

Turtles are amongst the oldest reptiles on the planet, offering a living link with the age of the dinosaurs. They can grow to up to 3m (10ft) in length, live more than 100 years, dive to depths of up to a kilometre and hold their breath for half an hour – as well as migrating for distances of up to 5,000km (3,000 miles).

like scenery which receives far less rainfall than the areas behind. The first of the area's two excellent national parks, **Bundala National Park** (open daily 6.30am–6.30pm; admission fee), is famous principally for the immensely varied aquatic and other bird life found in the park's coastal wetlands and lagoons. Almost 200 species of bird have been recorded here, including the prolific flocks of greater flamingos which arrive from northern India. A large population of wild peacocks adds a distinctive and colourful flourish to the park's tangled grey-green woodlands. Birds apart, Bundala is also home to a rich stock of wildlife including troupes of hyperactive grey langur monkeys, a small number of elephants and ferocious-looking crocodiles, plus sloth bears, civets, giant squirrels and the occasional leopard.

Tissamaharama and Yala

Beyond Bundala the coastal highway veers inland to reach the pleasant town of **Tissamaharama** (usually shortened to 'Tissa'). The town offers a convenient base for trips to Bundala and Yala National Parks, as well as the temple town of

Water buffalo at Yala

Kataragama, but is also of modest historical interest in its own right, occupying the site of the ancient former southern capital of Mahagama. A trio of large stupas strung across the town attest to its former importance, as does the beautiful **Tissa Wewa**, an artificial lake just north of the modern town centre created in the 2nd or 3rd century BC. For most visitors, however, Tissa's major attraction is its proximity to **Yala National Park** (open daily 6.30am–6.30pm; admission fee), one of the largest and certainly the most popular in Sri Lanka. The principal attraction here is leopards. Yala has one of the densest concentrations of these elegant and elusive felines anywhere in the world. There are also elephants, sloth bears, spotted deer, mongooses, porcupines and a compelling array of bird life, including peacocks and myriad colourful bee-eaters, bulbuls, hoopoes and parakeets.

Kataragama

Inland from Tissa lies the remote temple town of **Kataragama**, one of the island's most revered pilgrimage sites, held sacred by Buddhists, Hindus and Muslims alike. The town owes its importance to the presence here of the island's principal shrine to the god Kataragama, a deity of typically confused Sri Lankan lineage. Named after the town in which his shrine is located, Kataragama is seen by Sinhalese Buddhists as one of the island's four great protective deities. Sri Lankan Tamils regard him as a local manifestation of the great Hindu god Skanda, son of Shiva, lending the shrine a multi-faith significance which transcends strict ethnic and religious divides.

Kataragama's shrine, and that of other attendant deities, plus a large stupa and a mosque, occupy the so-called **Sacred Precinct**, a pleasant area of parkland populated by innumerable curious grey langur monkeys and separated from the modern town by the Menik Ganga, in whose waters pilgrims bathe before approaching the temple. The town and temple are comatose by day, but come dramatically alive during the nightly puja, with musicians, singers, dancers and crowds of pilgrims bowed down with huge bowls of fruit as offerings. The scene is at its most dramatic during the annual **Kataragama Festival**, when the god's more ecstatic followers perform gruesome acts of devotion and penance including walking across burning coals and piercing their flesh with long metal skewers.

Drummers at Kataragama

KANDY

Nestled amongst spectacular green mountains at the heart of the hill country, Kandy is the definitive Sri Lankan city, home to the country's most revered shrine, its most vibrant performing arts tradition and its greatest festival, the Esala Perahera *(see page 97)*. The last bastion of independent Sinhalese rule in Sri Lanka, the Kandyan Kingdom served as the crucible of the island's distinctive Sinhalese Buddhist culture, resisting repeated attacks by the Portuguese and Dutch before finally falling to the British in 1815. It still retains a slightly aristocratic sense of self-importance as the island's principal leader in traditional cultural values.

Kandy is now the island's second-largest city, but although there are crowds and traffic aplenty, the city's low-rise streets, numerous historic monuments and extensive

Kandy's lakeside Temple of the Tooth and other buildings

tracts of surrounding greenery lend it a refreshing small-town atmosphere compared with the great sprawl of Colombo. There is enough in the town and surrounding countryside to keep anyone occupied for weeks, ranging from Buddhist temples to elephant sanctuaries, and a visit of at least a day or two is an essential part of any tour of the island.

The Lake and Around

The centre of Kandy is dominated by the large artificial **lake**, created by the last king of Kandy, the infamous Sri Wickrama Rajasinha, using forced labour, although its placid waters give no hint of its unsavoury origins. Just south of the lake, the small **Royal Palace Park** offers fine views over the town and temples. There are even more extensive views from Rajapahilla Mawatha, a road that winds high above the southern side of the lake, giving incomparable panoramas across the city. The city centre, to the west of the lake, consists of a tight grid of busy streets overlooked by the vast **Bahiravakanda Buddha**, posed serenely on a hill overhead.

The dense green forest covering the steep hillside immediately behind the Temple of the Tooth is part of the beautiful **Udawattakele Sanctuary** (open daily 7am–5pm; admission fee), a miniature tropical wilderness almost in the centre of town which is home to a rich array of bird life, the occasional monkey and (if it has been raining) a considerable number of leeches. It is a beautiful spot, although the grossly inflated entrance charge levied on foreign tourists discourages visitors.

Temple of the Tooth

The **Temple of the Tooth**, or Dalada Maligawa (open daily 6am–8pm; admission fee), is home to Sri Lanka's most revered religious relic, the **Buddha's Tooth**, which attracts pilgrims from across the island, and indeed from many other Buddhist countries around Asia. Sitting on the north shore of the lake, the temple comprises a picturesque complex of neat white buildings topped with hipped roofs, framed against the luxuriant green slopes of the Udawattakele Sanctuary, and the entire ensemble is beautifully reflected in the waters of the lake.

Heavy security marks the approach to the temple, the result of an LTTE bomb attack in 1998 which badly damaged the facade. Beyond the various checkpoints, an elegant white outer wall and moat enclose the temple, while to the left is an eye-catching octagonal tower, the **Pittirippuva**, from which all new Sri Lankan heads of state address the nation.

Inside, the temple buildings cluster around a single, surprisingly small courtyard, in the middle of which stands the **Tooth Relic shrine**, ornately decorated with wall paintings, elephant

---

The Buddha's Tooth

One of the world's most revered Buddhist relics, the Buddha's Tooth was recovered from the master's funeral pyre at Kushinagar in north India in 543BC and, following the decline in Buddhism in India, smuggled into Sri Lanka in the 4th century AD. Once in Sri Lanka, the Tooth Relic developed into the defining symbol of Sinhalese sovereignty, so that whoever possessed it was believed to hold the right to rule the island, lending it a unique political as well as a spiritual importance. The Tooth Relic was first taken to Anuradhapura, then to Polonnaruwa, and then to various other places around the island before finally arriving in Kandy in 1592, where it became the focus of the massive Esala Perahera festival *(see page 97)*. Security concerns mean that the Tooth Relic is now only rarely put on display to the general public, though its appeal amongst Sri Lankan Buddhists remains undimmed. Its exact nature remains unclear, however – one sceptical Portuguese visitor suggested that its unusual size was due to the fact that it originally belonged to a buffalo.

tusks, richly carved stone pillars and three lavishly carved doors. The tooth itself is housed in a room on the upper storey of the shrine, which is opened for daily pujas at 6am, 10am and 7pm, a ceremony enlivened with exuberant Kandyan drumming. The tooth remains locked carefully away in an elaborate golden reliquary in the innermost room of the

Inside the Tooth Relic Shrine

shrine, and is shown only to the most important of visitors. At the rear of the courtyard, the modern **Alut Maligawa** shrine, built in 1956, houses a large collection of Buddha statues donated by Buddhists from all over the world. The rooms above this are home to the **Sri Dalada Museum** (additional admission fee), which is devoted to the Tooth Relic, and in particular to the large and eclectic selection of gifts presented as offerings to it over the centuries.

Royal Palace Complex

The Temple of the Tooth was formerly just one part of the **Royal Palace** complex, home to the kings of Kandy, whose surviving buildings enclose the temple and now house a sequence of museums. Exiting the temple to the north brings you to the imposing **Audience Hall**, a grand pavilion whose characteristic hipped roof is supported by dozens of lavishly carved wooden pillars – a classic example of open-plan Kandyan-style architecture. Just beyond here, a more modest building houses the **Raja Tusker Museum**, home to the stuffed remains of the much-loved Raja, a magnificent pachyderm which was until his death in 1988 the leading elephant in

Performances of Kandyan dancing and drumming are staged nightly at several venues around town – touristy but enjoyable spectacles in which sumptuously costumed dancers perform superbly acrobatic routines to an accompaniment of wildly energetic drum beats.

the city's famous Esala Perahera festival *(see page 97).*

To reach the remaining buildings of the Royal Palace, it is necessary to leave the temple and head outside along the shore of the lake. On the lakefront by the south side of the temple lies another striking Kandyan-style building, the two-storey **Queen's Bath** (Ulpenge). Immediately beyond is the extensive **National Museum, Kandy** (open Mon–Thur and Sun 9am–5pm; admission fee), which houses an extensive collection of antique Kandyan artefacts ranging from palm-leaf manuscripts to ivory jewellery. Continue away from the lake past the British courts to reach the **Archaeological Museum** (open Wed–Mon; admission with Cultural Triangle ticket – *see page 61* – or by donation). Housed in a fine old building which was formerly the king's palace, it is now home to a jumble of old stone carvings, pillars and pots. Finally, hidden behind the National Museum, the lovingly restored **Kandy Garrison Cemetery** is home to an atmospheric cluster of memorials to the city's early British inhabitants, the inscriptions on the headstones painting a vivid picture of the perils of life in the tropics in the 19th century.

▶ The Devales

The northern side of the Temple of the Tooth precinct is bounded by the atmospheric enclosures of the three devales (temples), dedicated to three of the four deities who are traditionally thought to protect the Kandyan kingdom (the fourth devale, an interesting little shrine dedicated to the god Kataragama, lies nearby in the city centre on Kotugodelle

Vidiya). Approached through a gateway to the left of the entrance to the Temple of the Tooth, the **Pattini Devale** is dominated by an enormous bo tree raised on a huge stone platform. The temple itself, a small but lavishly decorated building, stands just to the right of the entrance. Next to here is the Victorian **St Paul's Church**, an incongruous Anglican intrusion in this most sacred Buddhist precinct, whose beautifully preserved interior offers a moving memorial to the city's early British settlers.

Continue through the Pattini Devale to reach the **Natha Devale**, a quaint collection of stupas and shrines. Its principal shrine (on the south side of the enclosure), occupies a diminutive stone building, topped by an Indian-style *shikhara* dome, which is the oldest in Kandy. Heading left out of the Natha Devale brings you to the finest of the three devales, the **Vishnu Devale**, whose main building, approached via a long flight of steps, houses a wooden pavilion, or *digge*, traditionally used as a practice venue by the city's drummers and dancers.

Botanical Gardens

The countryside around Kandy offers several rewarding day trips. Just 6km (4 miles) outside the city, the

 very extensive **Peradeniya Botanical Gardens** (open

daily 8am–5pm; admission fee) are the finest in the country, home to a vast array of tropical flora set in a bend in the Mahaweli Ganga. The minimal signage means that non-botanists will struggle to get a full sense of what they are seeing, although the basic map available at the entrance gives a rough idea of the gardens' layout and content. From the entrance, the stately **Royal Palm Avenue** leads to the **Great Lawn**, where a massive Javan fig has created a kind of enormous arboreal pavilion, normally busy with picnicking locals. Beyond here, the northern section of the gardens is the wildest, home to an enormous population of fruit bats who hang in great clusters from the trees overhead.

Pinnewala Elephant Orphanage

An hour's drive west of Kandy lies one of the island's most popular attractions, the outstanding **Pinnewala Elephant Orphanage** (open daily 8.30am–6pm; admission fee), the world's largest collection of captive elephants. The orphanage is home to more than 60 animals orphaned or injured in the wild, mainly as a result of the innumerable clashes between elephants and villagers which, sadly, are an ongoing feature of life in the island – as well as an increasing number of elephants born here in captivity. The elephants range in age from the stately elderly matriarchs to the tiniest and cutest of baby pachyderms. Visits are best timed to coincide with the daily feeding and bathing sessions (10am–noon and 2–4pm). During the feeding sessions, the younger elephants are hand-fed from enormous bottles of milk, while twice daily the entire herd is driven down to the Ma Oya river to

> **Pinnewala's elephants include one blind elephant, Raja, and one with only three legs, christened Sama, who had the misfortune to step on a landmine laid during the civil war.**

Residents of the Elephant Orphanage

splash around in the water for an hour or so – a marvellous sight, despite the fact that the elephants are regularly out-numbered by the hordes of camera-toting tourists who congregate for the spectacle.

The only drawback to Pinnewala is that it is not possible to interact with the elephants, or to learn much about them. However, two other local elephant sanctuaries, although housing far fewer elephants, do offer tourists the chance to learn more about them. Close to Pinnewala, the **Millennium Elephant Foundation** (open daily 8am–5pm; admission fee), home to around eight elephants, is a good place to learn more about their role in Sri Lankan life and culture, and you can even offer your services in voluntary programmes to help the animals. Alternatively, the **Riverside Elephant Park** (open daily 7.30am–4.30pm; admission fee), just outside Kandy, offers the chance to ride one of the beasts, help to wash one or even go on a short elephant safari.

THE HILL COUNTRY

Occupying the southern heart of the island, the hill country is Sri Lanka at its most scenic: a magnificent region of precipitous green mountains carpeted with lush tea plantations and dotted with tumbling waterfalls and old-world British colonial memorabilia – gothic churches, half-timbered villas and rattling railways – which add a quaintly whimsical touch to the highlands' compelling natural attractions.

For most of the country's history this beautiful but rugged region was sparsely populated and, with the exception of the area around Kandy, of minimal political significance. But with the arrival of the British and the introduction of large-scale tea cultivation in the 19th century, the area assumed an increasing economic importance, one that it maintains to this day. The arrival of thousands of Indian

Adam's Peak in the southern hill country

Tamils (the so-called 'Plantation Tamils') to work the tea estates added a further splash of ethnic colour to this fascinating region.

Nuwara Eliya and Around

At the heart of the southern hill country lies the old colonial resort of **Nuwara Eliya**, the highest town in Sri Lanka, dominated by the densely forested bulk of **Pidurutalagala**, or Mount Pedro, the island's tallest peak at 2,555m (8,380ft) (although sadly the summit itself is off limits). First established by the British in the 19th century, Nuwara Eliya is often touted as Sri Lanka's 'Little England', and although much of the centre is now an unattractive mess of concrete buildings and smelly traffic, the open spaces of Victoria Park and the golf course add some welcome greenery to the modern centre. The edges of town still sport a fair sprinkling of atmospheric colonial-era villas and hotels whose incongruous architecture – a mix of fake-half timbering and brightly painted seaside-style architecture – add a pleasant touch of old-world whimsy. Many of the town's colonial-era buildings have now been converted into engagingly atmospheric hotels, most strikingly St Andrew's, the Grand and, most famously, the Hill Club, a venerable old stone building whose nostalgic interior offers a memorable glimpse of colonial life in the tropics.

The town also makes an excellent base for exploring the surrounding region, and has wonderful scenery in its immediate vicinity, most easily enjoyed by making the short walk up **Single Tree Mountain**, from where there are marvellous panoramas over the surrounding mountains. Slightly further afield are the **Hakgala Gardens**, set at the foot of the imposing Hakgala Rock. Established in 1861 as a place to grow cinchona, a source of the anti-malarial drug quinine, the gardens were later planted with an extensive range of local and foreign flora and offer a beautiful retreat from the hustle and bustle of Nuwara Eliya, as well as an excellent place to spot some of Sri Lanka's rare endemic montane bird species.

Nuwara Eliya also lies at the heart of the Sri Lankan tea industry, with mile upon mile of the surrounding hills carpeted in endless swathes of lush green tea bushes. Two local tea plantations welcome visitors: the **Pedro Tea Estate**, just 3km (2 miles) east of town, and the beautiful **Labookelie Estate** further away to the south. Both offer interesting factory tours and the chance to wander amongst the immaculately manicured surrounding plantations watching brightly attired female Tamil tea-pickers at work.

Sri Lankan Tea

The tea industry played a formative role in Sri Lanka's early commercial history, and although it has now been overtaken in importance by the garment-manufacturing and tourist industries, it retains a crucial role in the island's modern economy. Sri Lanka remains the world's second largest exporter of the beverage, after India, and the tea industry accounts for around a quarter of the country's export earnings. The suitability of the island's central highlands – with their wet, elevated and steeply shelving terrain – for tea growing was first recognised by the British, who began enthusiastically establishing plantations here following the collapse of the island's coffee industry in the second half of the 19th-century. Many of the factories and estates they established remain in operation to this day, still largely worked by the descendants of the original 'Plantation Tamils' who were brought by the British from India to address the labour shortage in the highlands. In general, the higher the plantation, the more delicate and sought-after the tea. The so-called 'high-grown' tea from the premier estates around Nuwara Eliya remains amongst the most highly prized in the world market today.

Horton Plains and World's End

The most memorable attraction within striking distance of Nuwara Eliya is **Horton Plains National Park** (open daily 6.30am–6.30pm; admission fee), lying on the very edge of the hill country. The plains are a world away from the humid lowlands: a bleak, mist-shrouded expanse of moorland, more reminis-

Harvesting the tea

cent of Scotland than a tropical island, dotted with strands of tangled cloud forest. At the southern edge of the park, the unforgettable viewpoint at **World's End** offers perhaps Sri Lanka's finest and most famous panorama (the unpredictable weather permitting; get there early), perched on the edge of a huge, sheer cliff face which plunges almost 1,000m (3,300ft) to the lowland plains below.

Haputale

East of Horton Plains, a string of small towns and villages sit atop the escarpment at the southern edge of the hill country, all offering magnificent views and scenery, extensive tea plantations, and occasional touches of colonial memorabilia. There are more stunning views from the ramshackle little town of **Haputale**, perched on the very edge of the hills, and memorable walks in the vicinity. The finest route heads out of town to the picturesque **Dambatenne Tea Factory** and its beautiful tea gardens, then climbs up to **Lipton's Seat**, named after the famous Victorian tea magnate whose name still adorns tea bags worldwide, and which is a serious rival to the better known World's End viewpoint.

Monks at Ella Falls

Ella and Around

Most visitors, however, press on to **Ella**: a charming little English-style village poised above **Ella Gap**, and offering further superlative views through a narrow cleft in the hills down to the plains below. The village itself is one of the most relaxing places in Sri Lanka to unwind for a few days, with a plethora of small, unassuming but enjoyable guesthouses serving up some of the best home cooking on the island. You can work up an appetite by tackling some of the wonderful walks through the surrounding tea plantations, most notably the short but rewarding hike up **Little Adam's Peak** and the longer, more challenging ascent of **Ella Rock**.

Ella is also a good base from which to explore the area's myriad attractions. Just below the village, the majestic **Rawana Ella Falls** tumble down a series of sheer cliff faces. This is one of the finest of the hill country's many waterfalls and one of several places around Ella named after Rawana, the demonic villain of the great Indian epic the *Ramayana*, who it is claimed imprisoned Rama's wife Sita in a cave nearby. After the Falls, the road hairpins dramatically down to the dog-eared little town of **Wellawaya**, which lies at the foot of the escarpment. Just beyond are the statues of **Buduruwagala**, a majestic sequence of seven figures carved in low relief into a towering rock face and showing, for Sri Lanka, an unusual selection of deities, including the Mahayana Buddhist deities Avalokitesvara and Maitreya alongside the Buddha himself.

Adam's Peak

At the opposite end of the southern hill country, west of Horton's Plains, the soaring summit of **Adam's Peak** towers high over the lowlands below. The mountain is both one of Sri Lanka's most dramatic natural features and also one of its most revered pilgrimage sites thanks to the small and curiously shaped depression on the summit that is popularly claimed to be the Buddha's Footprint, or **Sri Pada**. Not to be left out, the island's Hindus, Muslims and Christians subsequently came up with their own legends claiming that the footprint is that of Shiva, Adam and St Thomas respectively – though none of these claims has ever gathered much popular support.

During the pilgrimage season (Dec/Jan–May), thousands of pilgrims make the arduous ascent up the 4,800 steps that lead to the summit. Traditionally, the climb is made in the cool of the night in order to reach the summit by dawn. In

Adam's Peak, the perfect shadow, seen at dawn

season, the steps are illuminated and dotted with impromptu teashops offering refreshment to weary pilgrims. Not only does this night-time ascent offer the best odds of a cloud-free view from the top, but it also gives you the chance to see the peak's famous **shadow**, a perfectly triangular mirage cast by the summit, which seems to hang mysteriously in mid-air for 20 minutes or so following sunrise, weather permitting. Buddhists believe that this shadow is a physical representation of the 'Triple Gem', a kind of Buddhist Holy Trinity symbolising the Buddha, his teachings, and the Sangha (a community of Buddhist monks).

Ratnapura and Around

The town of Ratnapura lies directly south of Adam's Peak, though to reach it by road involves a long and circuitous road journey either south through Balangoda or northwest through the dramatic ranges at the western edge of the hill country to **Kitulgala**. Kitulgala is famous as the spectacular location for the filming of the Oscar-winning *The Bridge on the River Kwai* and is now a popular centre for white-water rafting on the choppy waters of the Kelani Ganga.

The sizeable town of **Ratnapura** itself is the largest in the region, pleasantly situated amidst the southern ranges of the hill country and famous as the centre of the island's gem-mining industry. Enormous quantities of precious stones are excavated by hand from the alluvial deposits washed down from the hills here using primitive and labour-intensive mining techniques.

You can watch uncut gems being traded in town along **Saviya Street** (though rip-offs are common, and it is best not to buy unless you are an expert gemologist), and it is also possible to arrange visits to local 'mines' (effectively just large holes in the ground) in order to watch local gem-diggers in action.

Uda Walawe and Sinharaja

For many visitors, however, the main attraction of Ratnapura is as a base from which to visit the two outstanding national parks nearby. The increasingly popular **Uda Walawe National Park** (open daily 6.30am–6.30pm; admission fee), is just south of the hill country. Although the park's arid and denuded landscape is relatively unimpressive, the lack of forest cover makes it one of the easiest places in the island to spot wildlife, such as elephants and a fine selection of birds, including many raptors.

West of Uda Walawe, draped over the undulating southern outliers of the hill country, **Sinharaja** (open daily 8am–6pm; admission fee) is quite unlike anywhere else on the island: a perfectly preserved tract of rainforest which has survived unscathed. The world inside the forest is positively Amazonian: trees, creepers, ferns, lianas and epiphytes, all tangled together in damp exuberance. As might be expected, the forest is a treasure box of ecological curiosities, including monkeys, reptiles, many rare endemic bird species and a baffling array of insect life, although the density of the vegetation and the height of the forest canopy makes wildlife-spotting surprisingly difficult without the services of a trained guide.

Sinharaja rainforest

THE CULTURAL TRIANGLE

The Aukana Buddha

North of the hill country stretch the plains of the northern dry zone, a great stretch of hot, denuded savannah, covered in thorny scrub and dotted with dramatic rocky outcrops. Despite the harshness of the natural environment, these plains were home to the remarkable civilisation of the ancient Sinhalese, which flourished here from around the 4th century BC until the 13th century AD. Their cultural, agricultural and architectural achievements ranked amongst the finest in the ancient world, until they were finally destroyed by repeated Tamil invasions.

Following the abandonment of the plains, the region's two great cities and innumerable smaller religious sites were largely abandoned to the jungle until they were recovered by 20th-century archaeologists. Their collective remains – a remarkable array of stupas, temples, palaces, monasteries and monolithic Buddha statues – offer a fascinating insight into the unique arts and culture of Sri Lanka's early Sinhalese people.

This area of the island is now commonly described as the **Cultural Triangle** (with the three points of the imaginary triangle being placed at the cities of Kandy, Anuradhapura and Polonnaruwa). This is a convenient modern tourist name for the region, although it is also, and more accurately, known by its ancient name of **Rajarata**, or 'The King's Land'.

North from Kandy to Dambulla

A handful of interesting sights dot the countryside between Kandy and Dambulla, including a trio of temples which merit a visit on the journey north. The first, right next to the main highway, just north of the town of Matale is **Alu Vihara**, an interesting Buddhist monastic complex featuring a sequence of cave temples hidden amidst enormous rock outcrops. The complex is famous mainly for being the place where the principal Buddhist scriptures, the *Tripitakaya*, were first written down, an event which had enormous significance in the international development of the religion.

Hidden away a few miles west of the highway in a beautiful rural location in the village of Ridigama, **Ridi Vihara** is one of the most interesting small temples on the island, housing a range of ancient sculptures and other rare artefacts. Back on the main road and continuing north, the exquisite little stone temple at **Nalanda** (admission fee, or free with CT ticket), was built as a Buddhist shrine, though in a style which is strongly reminiscent of Hindu Indian architecture, and even includes a couple of (very eroded) erotic carvings.

The Cultural Triangle Ticket

The Cultural Triangle (CT) Ticket covers most of the main Cultural Triangle sites, including Anuradhapura, Polonnaruwa and Sigiriya (but not Dambulla). The ticket is available from the main sites or from the CT offices in Kandy and Colombo; it costs $40 and is valid for one entry to each site for 14 days from first use. Buying a CT ticket makes good sense if you're visiting more than a couple of the area's principal attractions, since tickets for admission to individual sites can otherwise cost as much as $20.

Dambulla

North of Nalanda, the drab little town of Dambulla is home to the island's finest group of **rock temples** (open daily 7.30am–7pm; admission fee), nestling among a series of huge granite outcrops which tower over the southern end of town. There are five temples here, sitting side-by-side beneath a huge rocky overhang and filled with a veritable treasury of Buddhist art, including innumerable statues of the Buddha and other deities, plus the finest selection of murals on the island.

The finest of the rock temples, Caves 2 and 3, are masterpieces of Sinhalese art. Cave 3, the **Maha Alut Viharaya**, reaches a height of 10m (33ft), with a sloping roof which gives it the appearance of an enormous tent. As well as the cave's fine Buddha statues, some carved from solid rock, there are outstanding murals (look up as you enter the cave) showing the Buddha preaching and (to the left of the entrance) a statue of the Kandyan king Kirti Sri Rajasinha, who was largely responsible for the temples' 18th-century embellishments.

Even larger and finer is Cave 2, the **Maharaja Vihara**, a vast underground space some 50m (165ft) long and crammed full of a treasure box of Sri Lankan religious art, including more than a hundred Buddhas ranged around the walls

Maharajah Vihara at Dambulla

in various poses. There is also an eye-boggling collection of murals, including the extraordinary **Mara Parajaya**, showing the Buddha's defeat of Mara and his massed regiments of hairy demons; and the seductive **Daughters of Mara**, in which the Buddha is shown resisting the considerable attractions of the demon's legion of comely daughters.

Sigiriya

Sri Lanka's most remarkable single attraction, the spectacular citadel of **Sigiriya**, sits atop a vast gneiss outcrop which towers more than 200m (650ft) above the surrounding plains at the heart of the Cultural Triangle. The citadel was established in the 5th century by the infamous Kassapa, who murdered his father and assumed the kingship of the island, establishing a new and impregnable fortress-palace atop Sigiriya rock. He ruled the island from here for 18 years before being killed in battle, after which Sigiriya was abandoned.

The entire eastern side of the rock is surrounded by an extensive moat, past which an avenue arrows towards the rock, crossing a series of elaborate pleasure gardens. The first section, the **Water Gardens**, consists of an elaborate arrangement of pools and fountains, beyond which are the much more naturalistic **Boulder Gardens**, littered with massive rocks. Several of the caves found here were also home to reclusive monks, and still bear slight traces of murals, while some of the boulders have been carved into 'thrones' which probably had a symbolic religious significance.

The Water Gardens at Sigiriya

Past the Boulder Gardens, steps climb with increasing steepness up to the base of the rock itself. Close to the foot of the rock, a pair of incongruous Victorian metal spiral staircases lead up to the so-called **Sigiriya Damsels**, one of Sri Lanka's most famous sights: a little picture gallery showing around 20 beautiful bare-breasted nymphs floating on a sea of clouds. Immediately past the damsels, the pathway up the rock is flanked by the **Mirror Wall**, whose brightly polished surface is inscribed with hundreds of ancient graffiti messages recording early visitors' impressions of the site – and the nearby damsels in particular. Many are of considerable poetic value, and an important source for historians of Sinhalese language and script.

Further steps lead onwards and upwards to the **Lion Platform**, embellished with two enormous stone

Sigiriya Damsel

paws, all that remains of the open-mouthed lion which originally guarded the final ascent to the summit of the rock and Kassapa's palace. Metal steps lead between the paws and up to the summit, clinging to the bare rock face (and presenting something of a challenge to sufferers of vertigo). The summit itself is covered in the slight remains of Kassapa's palace, although the great jumble of brick foundations is difficult to interpret and far less impressive than the stupendous views down over the Water Gardens below and the plains stretching away in every direction.

Polonnaruwa

Another of Sri Lanka's great ruined cities, **Polonnaruwa** was capital of the island for a far shorter period of time. It enjoyed a brief but exuberant cultural flowering during its 150 years of pre-eminence from 1056 to 1215, during which Sinhalese art and architecture reached new heights of artistry. The **ruins** (open daily 7am–6pm; admission fee, or free with CT ticket)

Quadrangle

Polonnaruwa

0   1 km
0   1 mile
New Town

here are more compact, more varied and much more easily digestible than those at Anuradhapura, although it is also more of a museum piece and lacks something of Anuradhapura's enduring religious vibrancy.

Before entering the site itself, make time for the excellent **Polonnaruwa Museum** (open daily 9am–6pm; admission with CT ticket), the best in the island, with absorbing displays of artefacts from and information about life in the ancient city.

The Royal Palace

Close to the entrance, the **Royal Palace Group** comprises the substantial remains of the palace built by the city's most famous king, Parakramabahu the Great (reigned 1153–86), who was responsible for many of the city's most impressive structures, though his lust for building and weakness for ill-advised military campaigns almost bankrupted the kingdom. The remains of the **Royal Palace** itself are large but rather plain. More impressive is the **Council Chamber**, the king's audience hall, whose finely carved base is decorated with dwarfs and galloping elephants and topped with a pair of superb lion statues – the defining symbol of Sinhalese royalty. Just northeast of here, look out for the finely preserved **Royal Baths**.

The Quadrangle

Contained in a small enclosure just north of the Royal Palace is the remarkable cluster of buildings known as the **Quadrangle**. This was the religious heart of the city, home to the famous Tooth Relic *(see page 46)*, which was housed here in various temples. The finest of these is the magnificent **Vatadage**, probably the most beautiful building in Sri Lanka, a glorious circular structure decorated in a riot of carving, with four sumptuous staircases, each embellished with a

The Vatadage at Polonnaruwa

> Hiring a bicycle is the most enjoyable way to explore Polonnaruwa. The flat, traffic-free roads through the site make it one of Sri Lanka's most enjoyable two-wheel experiences.

moonstone, and a *makara*-decorated balustrade.

Numerous other remains stand cheek-by-jowl around the enclosure. The most obviously impressive is the **Thuparama**, a solid and unusually well preserved structure whose exterior carvings show distinct Hindu influence, the result of the powerful coterie of Tamil mercenaries and other Indians who made the city their home. Other notable buildings include the **Hatadage**, another temple which once housed the Tooth Relic; the uniquely Khmer-style **Satmahal Prasada**; the beautiful **Lotus Madapa** pavilion; and the enormous **Gal Pota**, a huge rock inscription recording the real and imagined exploits of Nissanka Malla, a famously boastful Polonnaruwan king whose self-glorifying inscriptions can be found all over the city. Immediately south of the Quadrangle is the very Indian-looking **Shiva Devale No. 1**, one of many Hindu temples at the site, built by the Tamil Pandyans who conquered the city in the 13th century.

The Alahana Pirivena and Beyond

North of the Quadrangle lie the extensive remains of the **Alahana Pirivena**, the city's most important monastery. The first notable sight here is the monumental **Rankot Vihara**, the only stupa at Polonnaruwa to rival the great examples at Anuradhapura. Continuing north, the heart of the monastery is marked by a cluster of exceptional buildings, including the **Lankatilake**, a narrow shrine enclosing a huge – though headless – standing Buddha; the **Kiri Vihara**, a fine, delicately built stupa; and the **Buddha Seema Pasada**, the monastery's chapter house. Finest of all, however, is the **Gal**

Vihara, further north, one of the island's most famous shrines, comprising a line of four monumental stone Buddhas including a vast reclining Buddha, the most famous statue in Sri Lanka, and, next to it, a unique standing figure with arms crossed who is sometimes thought to represent Ananda, the Buddha's most devoted follower *(see picture on page 14)*.

Continuing north, you pass the gargantuan **Demala Maha Seya** stupa, almost buried in vegetation, before reaching the **Tivanka-Patamaghara**, another Buddhist shrine built in a heavily Indianised architectural style, exemplified by the finely carved niched windows which decorate its exterior. Inside, a sequence of outstanding (though difficult to see) frescoes of Hindu-style deities in elaborate tiaras cover the walls.

A Buddhist monk

The Southern Remains

Further interesting remains lie south of the main site along the shores of the vast **Parakrama Samudra**, one of the greatest of the enormous artificial lakes, or 'tanks', built for irrigation by the ancient Sinhalese *(see page 74)*. The so-called **Rest House Group**, almost in the middle of the little modern town centre, comprises the modest remnants of Nissanka Malla's palace, while further south lies the **Potgul Vihara**, a circular shrine, and the famous statue of a bearded figure holding a palm-leaf manuscript, either a sage or Parakramabahu himself, depending on who you believe.

Minneriya and Kaudulla

If you have had enough of Buddhist remains, a pair of outstanding national parks lie close to Polonnaruwa. **Minneriya** and **Kaudulla National Parks** (both open daily 6.30am–6.30pm; admission fee) are famous mainly for their extensive elephant populations. The parks form part of an 'elephant corridor', and the animals migrate seasonally between the two reserves, depending on water levels in the local tanks (local guides will be able to tell you which of the two parks offers the best elephant-spotting opportunities at any given time). Elephants apart, the parks are also home to the usual range of Sri Lankan fauna including monkeys, sambur, spotted deer and numerous birds.

Elephant in the National Park

Yapahuwa to Ritigala

On the eastern edge of the Cultural Triangle, the ruined citadel of **Yapahuwa** (open daily 8am–6pm; admission fee) is all that remains of one of the many short-lived Sinhalese capitals which were established and then abandoned in rapid succession during the chaotic 13th and 14th centuries. The royal palace formerly stood atop

the enormous rocky outcrop
which forms the centrepiece
of the site, although the
main attraction is the spectacular **stone staircase**
which climbs up the rock
with dizzying steepness, and
is sumptuously decorated
with statues of elephants,
dwarfs, goddesses and a pair
of pop-eyed stone lions. The

> A legend states that the
> Aukana Buddha was
> carved by a master
> sculptor and the
> Sasseruwa Buddha by
> his apprentice – and
> that the student, on see-
> ing the excellence of his
> teacher's creation,
> abandoned his own
> statue in despair.

remains of a few other buildings and a small **museum** stand
at the foot of the steps.

Northeast of Yapahuwa is the **Aukana Buddha** (admission
fee, *see picture on page 60*), a 12-m (39-ft) high statue of a
standing Buddha which has become one of Sri Lanka's most
famous icons – a mighty and austerely simple figure, best seen
at dawn when the low light reveals the stone's fine detail (the
name Aukana means 'sun-eating'). Nearby is the equally grand
Sasseruwa Buddha (admission fee), another monumental, if
slightly less finely carved, standing figure – although for many
visitors the relative lack of sculptural finish makes it the more
humanised and endearing of the two colossi.

Continuing northeast you come to the atmospheric forest
monastery of **Ritigala** (admission fee, or free entry with CT
ticket), the best known of the various woodland retreats to
which the island's more ascetic monks withdrew in centuries
past. Buried amongst beautiful lowland dry-zone forest, the
monastery's ruins are deeply atmospheric but little understood, consisting of a succession of interlinked courtyards,
walkways and the foundations of structures built in a distinctive 'double-platform' style, with pairs of buildings surrounded by miniature moats and linked by tiny bridges –
although their exact function remains obscure.

Anuradhapura

Anuradhapura

At the northern edge of the Cultural Triangle, the great ruined city of **Anuradhapura** was for some 1,500 years the island's capital and cultural fulcrum. One of the greatest monastic cities the world has ever seen, ancient Anuradhapura supported a population of as many as 10,000 monks, and the ruins of its great religious foundations, monumental stupas and enormous man-made lakes continue to inspire awe amongst visitors and pride amongst the island's latter-day Sinhalese.

Most (but not all) of the main sites in Anuradhapura are contained in the so-called **Sacred Precinct**, to the west of the modern town of Anuradhapura, and are covered by the Cultural Triangle Ticket *(see page 61)*. The best way to see the sights is to hire a bicycle, although you will need a couple of days just to cover the main attractions, and far longer if you want to really get to understand the vast and often bewildering sprawl of monuments and ruins which dot the countryside in and around the city.

The Mahavihara

At the centre of the Sacred Precinct are the remains of the great **Mahavihara monastery**, still one of the island's great pilgrimage centres thanks to the presence here of the **Sri Maha Bodhi** (Sacred Bo Tree; donation), a tree of enormous age which was allegedly grown from a cutting from the tree in India under which the Buddha attained enlightenment. The Sri Maha Bodhi is now the focus of worship in Anuradhapura, and always busy with pilgrims and tourists alike.

North of the Sri Maha Bodhi rises the huge, dirty-white hemisphere of the **Ruvanvalisaya**, the third largest – and best preserved – stupa in the city, standing in a square compound whose flanking walls are decorated with dozens of elephant heads. From here a road runs north to another stupa, the **Thuparama**, the oldest in the whole of Sri Lanka and a far more modest structure than the Ruvanvalisaya, picturesquely framed by a cluster of lopsided columns which once supported a roof.

The Jetavana Monastery and the Citadel

Another of Anuradhapura's great monasteries, the **Jetavana**, lies just under a kilometre northeast of the Mahavihara. Like the Mahavihara, it is centred around a monumental **stupa**, a colossal brick edifice which once reached a height of 120m (390ft), though it has now been reduced to around 70m (230ft). It remains the world's largest brick-built structure. The area around the stupa is littered with remains, including

---

Irrigation in Ancient Sri Lanka

The trio of lakes which surround Anuradhapura are just three of the thousands of man-made reservoirs – or 'tanks' *(wewas)* – that dot Sri Lanka's northern plains. Early Sinhalese civilisation was agricultural, and the lack of regular rainfall in the northern dry zone meant that the storage and distribution of water from the region's few dependable rivers or collected during the brief monsoon, was crucial. The island's first reservoirs and irrigation channels date from the earliest days of Sinhalese settlement, but it was between the 3rd and 7th centuries AD that the vast system of tanks was linked by thousands of miles of irrigation channels in one of the greatest hydraulic achievements the world has seen. Over time, the maintenance of these systems began to place an untenable burden on the population and as waves of Tamil invaders harassed the north, they felt into disarray. Gradually, the water supply failed and the Sinhalese decamped, abandoning the northern plains and moving towards the less arid lands further south.

The enormous Jetavana stupa

a finely preserved bathing pool and the unusual 'Buddhist railing', a kind of ancient stone fence. There is also an interesting **museum** (open daily 8am–5pm, entrance free with CT ticket) housing an excellent selection of finely crafted items found at the site.

North of the Jetavana, the large walled area known as the **Citadel** formerly enclosed the city's royal palace and central commercial district, though little now survives apart from innumerable brick foundations of unidentifiable buildings and the remnants of the **Royal Palace** itself, notable mainly for the pair of fine guard stones at its entrance, showing a pair of unusually fat dwarves.

The Abhayagiri Monastery

Continuing north you come to the **Abhayagiri** monastery, once the largest in Anuradhapura, but now the least visited and therfore most atmospheric area in the city, with a prodi-

Et Pokuna, the Elephant Pool

gious quantity of foundations, pillars, staircases and eroded brick walls dotted amidst beautiful woodland. Again, a monumental **stupa** lies at the heart of the monastery, still largely unrestored and covered in a thick layer of vegetation. East of the stupa, the famous **Samadhi Buddha** statue shows the Buddha deep in meditation – a classic Sri Lankan pose, combining simplicity and serenity. Just beyond here are the marvellously well-preserved **Kuttam Pokuna**, two bathing pools which were once used for monks' ritual ablutions.

Further monuments lie scattered in the surrounding woodlands, including **Mahasen's Palace**, home to perhaps the finest moonstone in Sri Lanka; the **Ratna Prasada**, notable for its remarkable guard stone figure; and the gargantuan **Et Pokuna**, or Elephant Pool, the largest bathing pool in the city, and every bit as big as its name suggests.

Outlying Remains

A further rewarding clutch of monuments lies south of the Mahavihara, starting with the fine **Mirisavatiya Daboga**, a large white structure confusingly similar in size and appearance to the nearby Ruvanvalisaya, which is famous for having been built by King Dutugemunu out of remorse for having thoughtlessly eaten a bowl of chillies without offering any to the city's monks. South of here, the picturesque **Royal Pleasure Gardens** contain two fine bathing pools, one carved with wonderfully naturalistic low-relief elephants. Just beyond is the **Isurumuniya Vihara** (admission fee; not included in CT ticket), one of the oldest shrines in the city and home to an interesting selection of carvings.

Mihintale

Twelve kilometres (7 miles) east of Anuradhapura, **Mihintale** is revered amongst Sri Lankans as the place at which Buddhism was first introduced to the island. According to legend, it was here that Mahinda, and envoy of the great Indian Buddhist emperor Asoka, converted the Sinhalese king **Devanampiya Tissa** and his followers in 247BC. The site is deeply atmospheric, with a sequence of stupas and other remains scattered across a sequence of hilltops linked by beautiful stone stairways and shaded by innumerable frangipane trees.

After the car park, the site **museum** (open Wed–Mon) and the ruins of a medieval hospital, steps lead up to the remains of the **Medamaluwa monastery**. The remains include two huge stone troughs which would have originally been filled daily by devotees with rice for the monastery's monks, and a pair of ancient stone tablets on which are written the rules of monastic life. From here, a long line of steps leads to the centre of Mihintale (admission fee) and the small **Ambasthala Stupa**, allegedly marking the exact spot at which Mahinda converted Devanampiya Tissa. Steps lead from here to a cluster of further remains, including the dramatic **Aradhana Gala** rocky outcrop, from which Mahinda preached his first sermon, and up again to the **Mahaseya Stupa**, from where there are marvellous views out over the surrounding plains to the great stupas of Anuradhapura, clearly visible in the distance.

THE EAST

Sri Lanka's east is one of the poorest and most sparsely populated regions on the island thanks to its arid climate and inhospitable terrain. The area's fortunes were further blighted by the civil war, whose fluctuating front line ran through the region and pitted its inhabitants – a varied mix of Tamils, Sinhalese and Muslims – against one another in recurrent bouts of communal blood-letting, and by the Asian tsunami in 2004, which wreaked havoc all along the coast. For the visitor, the region's major attractions are at present limited to a handful of beaches and the little city of Trincomalee, the region's battered but personable capital.

Trincomalee

The principal city of the east, **Trincomalee** (or 'Trinco'), is Sri Lanka's most ethnically diverse city, its population divided almost equally between Tamils, Sinhalese and Muslims. Repeated clashes between these different ethnic groups made the city the most volatile in the island throughout the civil war, and have continued to overshadow its fortunes during the subsequent ceasefire. Although parts of the city are without doubt scruffy and unappealing, its multi-ethnic cultural mix, magnificent natural setting and faded colonial atmosphere lend it an understated but palpable charm.

Lover's Leap was named in honour of a young Dutch lady named Francina van Rhede who, according to tradition, jumped off it after having been abandoned by her lover – although colonial records suggest that not only did she survive the fall, but that she also subsequently married someone else.

Trinco's most interesting area, occupying a narrow promontory dividing Dutch

Lover's Leap on the Swami Rock

and Back bays, is **Fort Frederick**, the old colonial fort, surrounded by substantial old ramparts enclosing a tranquil
stretch of parkland dotted with old colonial buildings. Entering through the impressive main gate, a road winds up
through the fort to **Swami Rock**, a dramatic cliff top rising
high at the edge of the promontory above deep-blue waters,
with fine views over Back Bay, the town, and the innumerable fishing boats bobbing in the waters below. Perched atop
Swami Rock, the **Koneswaram Kovil** is one of the island's
holiest Shiva temples, although the building itself is modern
and of little interest. Immediately behind the temple, the
sheer cliff plunges into the waters at **Lover's Leap**.

Below Swami Rock, the town centre comprises a dusty
grid of low-rise streets dotted with colourful little Hindu
temples, with pleasant backstreets of decaying colonial villas. At the southeastern end of the centre, the dusty open
space of the Esplanade backs the attractive town beach

East coast beach

flanking Dutch Bay. Walking across the town centre brings you to **Inner Harbour**, the original source of the city's maritime prosperity and importance and still a grand sight, with large container ships and tanks moored in the distance and lines of hills beyond.

Uppaveli and Nilaveli

Most visitors come to the Trincomalee area to visit the twin resorts of **Uppaveli** and **Nilaveli**, lying on a swathe of beautiful golden sand a few kilometres north of the city. Despite repeated upheavals during the civil war and, more recently, significant tsunami damage, both resorts have somehow kept going against the odds, embodying the sense of enduring optimism which characterises life in the war-torn east and north.

Development is at present confined to a couple of large resort hotels and a cluster of low-key guesthouses, and the atmosphere is thoroughly somnolent. The main attractions besides lolling on the beach are the two tiny islets lying just offshore from Nilaveli. **Pigeon Island** was formerly fringed by a beautiful coral reef, which has now largely been destroyed, although the surrounding waters are still home to a substantial population of tropical fish. The corals fringing **Coral Island**, however, remain largely intact – so far, at least – and offer the island's most rewarding snorkelling, while diving can also be arranged from operators at both resorts.

Arugam Bay and Around

The east's most popular tourist destination, the village of **Arugam Bay** is Sri Lanka's premier surfing destination. Lying near the southern end of the east coast, the waves here are the finest on the island, and attract a steady stream of die-hard wave-chasers.

Surfing apart, Arugam Bay is the jumping off point for visits to two of Sri Lanka's lesser-known national parks: the small but beautiful **Lahugala** (open daily 6.30am–6.30pm; admission fee), home to a significant elephant population; and **Yala East** (open daily 6.30am–6.30pm; admission fee), which adjoins the far better known Yala National Park (although it is impossible to travel directly between the two) and is home to a broadly similar range of wildlife and bird life, although the park's flora and fauna has yet to recover from damage sustained in the civil war.

Coconut palm

THE NORTH

The north is Sri Lanka's least known and least developed region. Out of bounds during the two decades of civil war, the area only reopened to visitors following the ceasefire in 2001 and remains almost completely untouched by modern tourism. Not that the region is without attractions. Home to an almost exclusively Tamil population, the north is quite unlike the rest of Sri Lanka, and its long history has blended Hindu, Christian and colonial traditions into a unique whole.

Jaffna

For visitors accustomed to the Sinhalese south, the historic old Tamil city of **Jaffna** offers an entirely different perspective on Sri Lanka. The crucible of Tamil culture on the island, the city looks for inspiration as much to India, a short distance north over the Palk Straits, as to Colombo, and retains a character quite different from that in the rest of the island. Repeatedly besieged and fought over during the civil war, parts of Jaffna still bear the signs of conflict, most notably in the area around the huge Dutch **fort**, the largest in Asia. Much of the city, however, has survived surprisingly intact. The town centre remains vibrant and colourful, dotted with expansive Hindu temples and huge churches, and in the suburbs, decaying old Dutch villas still line the sedate, tree-lined streets. On the northern edge of town, the majestic **Nallur Kandaswamy Temple** is the most majestic Hindu temple in Sri Lanka, and the only one which rivals the great temples of India in size and in the intensity of its religious rituals and festivals.

The Jaffna Peninsula and Islands

Surrounding Jaffna at the northernmost point of Sri Lanka, the **Jaffna Peninsula** was for centuries the breadbasket of Jaffna city. Densely populated and agriculturally fertile, the

Jaffna street scene

peninsula has long been intensively settled, and is home to a cluster of low-key but interesting sights, ranging from the war-damaged temples of **Naguleswaram** and **Maviddapuram**; the hot springs of **Keerimalai**; the ancient cluster of miniature stupas at **Kantharoadai**; the village of **Velvettiturai** ('VVT'), birthplace of the infamous LTTE supremo Prabakaran; and the remarkable sand dunes of the **Manalkadu Desert**; as well as a smattering of little-visited beaches.

East of Jaffna, the shallow waters of the Jaffna lagoon are dotted with a string of beautiful islands, on which can be found further mementos of the region's long and intriguing history, including the Dutch forts of Urundi and Hammenhiel at **Kayts**; the temples of **Nainativu**; and finally the remote outpost of **Delft**, home not only to an unusual population of wild ponies, but also to a colonial fort and even a rare African baobab tree, thought to have been planted by the Portuguese.

WHAT TO DO

SHOPPING

Sri Lanka isn't quite the shopper's paradise of nearby India, Thailand or Indonesia. The island does churn out a lot of handicrafts, but sadly much of it is poor-quality tourist tat, exemplified by the third-rate suitcase-fillers sold at the government-run Laksala chain, which has shops in all the main towns around the island. There *is* interesting stuff to be found, however, if you are prepared to hunt around. The best places are Colombo, Kandy and the west coast resorts. Bargaining is the order of the day in all places except in the smartest shops – a request for a 'small discount' or 'special price' can work in many situations, especially if you are buying several items or making a big purchase, while at the more informal little shops and stalls you can usually haggle to your heart's content.

Handicrafts and Souvenirs

The most characterful Sri Lankan souvenirs are the brightly painted masks which are sold all over the country, especially along the west coast – the best selection can be found at Ambalangoda, the centre of the island's mask making industry. Size and quality vary enormously: from the minute to the huge, and from sloppily painted junk to meticulously crafted heirlooms. Elephant carvings are also ubiquitous, in wood, metal or stone, as well as elephant paintings and batiks, stuffed toy elephants, elephant jigsaws and so on. Again, quality varies widely. Next in popularity come Buddha carvings, in a similarly wide range of media and quality.

Bird batik, Aluvihara

Jewellery shop hoarding in the Pettah, Colombo

Metalwork (a speciality of the Kandy area) is popular, though the island's trays, candlesticks, plates and carvings can be a bit ornate for western tastes. Batik painting (introduced by the Dutch from Indonesia) is also fairly common. Most pieces feature naff tropical beach scenes, elephants or the Sigiriya Damsels, though a few places turn out more unusual stuff. Reasonable leatherwork and lacquerware is also available in a few places. For something more unusual you could look out for Kandyan drums, carrom boards, monks' begging bowls and robes or religious kitsch, such as the colourful posters of gods, which are sold all over the island.

Finally, a number of shops in Colombo offer chic contemporary takes on traditional handicrafts. Places to try include Paradise Road, Suriya, Elephant Corridor, the shop at the Gallery Café and, best of all, the celebrated Barefoot, whose signature hand-woven cotton textiles are used in the making

Tea and Spices

There is plenty of tea for sale in Sri Lanka, either in dedicated tea shops (Mlesna is the main chain) or in general shops and supermarkets (Cargills supermarkets usually have a good stock), though the range is often fairly limited. You might also want to stock up on cheap spices from local shops – though spices sold in the island's myriad spice gardens are usually massively marked up.

of all sorts of vibrantly coloured objects, from clothes and tablecloths to stationery and cuddly toys.

Gems and Jewellery

Sri Lanka's fame as a major international source of high-quality precious stones is reflected in the large number of gem and jewellery shops which dot the island's major tourist haunts. Shopping around may turn up some modest bargains, though unless you are an expert gemologist, stick to reputable shops and make sure you have done your homework so that you are able to compare prices and quality in Sri Lanka with those in your home country. Needless to say, buying gems from touts or street traders (such as those who hang around Ratnapura, the island's main gem-producing centre) is asking for trouble unless you really know your stuff.

Mask painting at Ariyapala and Sons Mask Museum

ENTERTAINMENT

Sri Lanka is badly lacking in nightlife. The island's only established nightclubs are found exclusively in Colombo – all are attached to big hotels and none is particularly special (with the exception of the stylish little Blue Elephant club at the Hilton hotel). It is probably better to head to one of the city's handful of fashionable bars, pubs and live-music venues, all of which can stay lively till late and are the best place to rub shoulders with the city's Eurocentric smart-set and sozzled expats. The liveliest places on the coast are Hikkaduwa and Unawatuna, though even here things are pretty sleepy – quiet late-night beers on the beach and Bob Marley are the order of the day (or night) here, rather than full-moon raves and drug-fuelled debauchery. Negombo also boasts a few lively bars in season, but away from these places, you can pretty much forget it.

Kandyan dance performers

After-hours entertainment is also largely non-existent. Colombo has a couple of cinemas and a smattering of cultural events, but that is about it. In Kandy, be sure to sample one of the shows of Kandyan dancing and drumming which are staged nightly at various venues around town – all are thoroughly touristy but undeniably fun, with acrobatic dancing, exuberant drumming and fire-walking guaranteed.

Cricket, a national obsession

SPORTS AND RELAXATION

Cricket

As in India and Pakistan, cricket is a national obsession In Sri Lanka – it is impossible to go far without seeing kids playing games with improvised bats and balls on any available bit of space, and matches featuring the national team are followed avidly by virtually every man and boy on the island. Test matches and one-day internationals are held in Colombo, Kandy and Galle (although the Galle cricket ground is currently out of service due to tsunami damage), while Dambulla also hosts one-day internationals.

Golf

Increasing numbers of tourists are taking advantage of the island's three beautiful 18-hole golf courses (all over 5,460m or 6,000yds; par 70–73), which can be found in Colombo, Kandy and Nuwara Eliya – the last two are particularly scenic. All three courses welcome casual visitors, and green fees and club hire are an absolute bargain compared with most other courses around the world.

Swimming

Splashing around into the warm waters of the Indian Ocean is one of the great pleasures of a visit to Sri Lanka. It is worth bearing in mind, however, that swimming conditions vary enormously around the coast, even within quite small distances along individual beaches, and there are strong currents and undertows in places, so it is always worth seeking local advice if you want to swim off a deserted section of beach – a depressing number of Sri Lankan lives are lost through drowning every year, as well as a small but significant number of tourists' lives. Be very careful if you are on the coast during the monsoon when seas can be rough.

Diving

Although not on a par with the nearby Maldives, Sri Lanka has a good range of diving sites and a well-established network of PADI diving schools around most parts of the coast. The island's marine environment is far from pristine, especially on the west coast, but although many of the offshore reefs have suffered significant damage, the coastal waters still boast abundant marine life, interesting underwater rock and cave formations and (on the west and south coasts) a large number of rewarding wreck dives. Most of the island's diving schools are situated on the west coast, mainly in the Bentota area and at Hikkaduwa; there are also schools on the south coast at Unawatuna and Weligama, and on the east coast at Uppaveli and Nilaveli.

The diving season runs from November to April on the west and south coasts, and from May to October on the east coast.

Surfing at Midigama on the south coast

Snorkelling

There is very little good snorkelling in Sri Lanka, and most of the reefs close to the shore have been seriously damaged. The best spots are at Coral Island, at Nilaveli on the east coast, and at Polhenu on the south coast (which has the added bonus of a couple of expert local snorkelling guides, contactable via the village's guesthouses). The Coral Gardens in Hikkaduwa also offer decent snorkelling and plenty of tropical fish, but are rather spoilt for snorkellers by the number of boats whizzing around.

Surfing

There are several excellent surf spots around the Sri Lankan coast. The island's premier surfing destination is Arugam Bay, which is internationally famous for its waves (best from May to October), offering a variety of breaks suitable for all standards from novice to expert. The other two main surfing destinations are Midigama on the south coast, and Hikkaduwa on the west coast (both best from November to April). There are specialist surfing shops at Arugam Bay and Hikkaduwa which offer tuition, board rental and repairs, and which also organise surf safaris to breaks along the coast. Boards can also be hired from a couple of guesthouses in Midigama, and on the beach at Unawatuna, where the more modest waves attract a fair number of local surfers, though relatively few foreigners.

Other Watersports

The water sports capital is Bentota, where the placid waters of the Bentota lagoon provide the perfect spot for all sorts of water-based fun, including windsurfing, water-skiing, jet-skiing, speed-boating, banana-boating, tube-riding, kayaking and lagoon boat trips (all of which can be organised through the resort's myriad water sports centres – try the Sunshine Watersport Centre in Aluthgama). The best spot for white-water rafting is Kitulgala, on the southwestern edge of the hill country, where the choppy Kelani Ganga river (famous as the location for the film *The Bridge on the River Kwai*) provides boulder-strewn stretches of grade 3–4 rapids.

Trekking and Cycling

The island's vast potential for activity holidays remains largely unexploited, though things are slowly changing. The hill country, in particular, is a walkers' paradise, with stunning scenery and a pleasantly temperate climate, though the lack of established long-distance hiking trails means that it's best to sign up with a local tour operator rather than attempting to strike out on your own. Cyclists have thousands of miles of relatively traffic-free minor roads to explore, though again it's probably easiest to take a tour with an established local operator – Adventure Sports Lanka and Jetwing Eco-

Holidays *(see pages 116–17)* are the two best for both hiking and cycling, as well as other activity holidays.

Wildlife

Sri Lanka has an outstanding collection of national parks covering large swathes of the island and boasting a fascinating array of wildlife. For most visitors the main attraction is the elephants, which can be seen in almost all the island's national parks, while the island's superb leopards are also a major draw, most easily seen at Yala National Park, which has one of the world's highest concentrations of this

Playful monkeys

elusive mammal. Various species of monkey, cute sloth bears, several types of deer, buffalo, wild boar, assorted squirrels, crocodiles and large monitor lizards are also commonly seen, while rarer and more reclusive species such as porcupine, fishing cats and mongooses can occasionally be spotted.

Sri Lanka is also one of Asia's premier bird-watching locations, boasting a vast range of colourful avifauna which appeals both to casual visitors and seasoned ornithologists alike. The island's wide range of natural habitats – from coastal wetlands to cloud forest – supports a uniquely varied array of resident bird life, while its equatorial location also attracts a wide range of seasonal migrants from as far away as Europe. More than 230 resident species have been recorded, including 33 endemic species which are found only on the island.

Yoga and Meditation

Yoga courses and facilities are less well established in Sri Lanka than in neighbouring India, although increasing numbers of ayurveda centres now offer yoga sessions either on their own or as part of treatment courses. Aficionados might consider a visit to Ulpotha (<www.ulpotha.com>), a specialist yoga retreat in the Cultural Triangle which attracts top international teachers for its two-week residential courses, though at top international prices.

The best place to study meditation is Kandy, which has a number of well-established centres. The best for foreign visitors is the Nilambe Meditation Centre (tel: 081-222 5471), in a beautiful setting high in the hills about 20km (12 miles) outside the city. There is no minimum or maximum length of stay, and the cost is just a few dollars a day, which includes basic lodging and food, though you will be expected to help out around the centre to pay for your keep and tuition.

Ayurveda

The traditional system of holistic health care known as Ayurveda (from the Sanskrit, meaning 'the science of life') has been practised in India and Sri Lanka for centuries. According to the Ayurvedic system, all bodies are made up of varying combinations of the five basic elements (ether, fire, air, earth and water) and governed by three *doshas* (*pitta*, *vata* and *kapha*), each of which is a combination of two or three of the five elements. Illnesses are seen simply as the result of an imbalance in the doshas, and so rather than treating illnesses and symptoms in isolation, Ayurveda aims to treat the whole patient, often trying to encourage a more balanced lifestyle.

A huge number of places (mainly in the west coast resorts) now offer Ayurveda treatments. These are basically of two types. Serious Ayurveda resorts and clinics cater for visitors (often with chronic medical problems) who go for long-term courses of treatment; these typically involve an individually prescribed Ayurvedic regimen of massages, baths and other treatments in combination with a quiet, alcohol-free and usually vegetarian lifestyle, all under the supervision of a trained Ayurveda doctor.

Far more common, however, are so-called 'soft' Ayurveda treatments, most commonly various forms of massage, herbal and steam baths, and *shirodhara*, which involves dribbling hot oil on the forehead (or 'third eye'). Although they are extremely pleasurable, these are essentially glorified de-stress and beauty treatments rather than genuine medical therapies. The massive boom in 'soft' Ayurveda over the past decade has recently encouraged many of the smarter west-coast hotels to open sumptuous new spas, in which 'soft' Ayurveda treatments are offered alongside mainstream spa treatments such as wraps and body polishes, facials, reflexology and aromatherapy treatments, and various forms of international-style massages such as Thai and Swedish.

Ayurvedic massage oil

CHILDREN'S SRI LANKA

The beach is likely to provide the main entertainment for kids visiting Sri Lanka, with mile upon mile of golden sand to muck around on and warm waters to dip into – though parents should always check local swimming conditions *(see page 90)* and be attentive to the very real dangers of sunburn and dehydration. Away from the coast, the country's top children's attraction is the Elephant Orphanage at Pinnewala, whose elephants are a guaranteed hit, especially the cute babies – one of the very few places in the world where kids can see elephants which are even smaller than themselves. There are further elephant sanctuaries around Kandy and at the Uda Walawe National Park, while a rattling jeep ride around any of the island's other national parks in search of elephants, leopards or other wildlife is also fun.

Older kids will enjoy some of the island's activity sports, such as water sports at Bentota or white-water rafting at Kitulgala *(see page 92)*. A tuktuk ride, a train trip through the hill country or a boat trip on one of the island's rivers or lagoons, or even in a fishing boat along the coast, should also appeal, while those with a head for heights might also fancy the challenge of clambering up Sigiriya.

Children in Ratnapura

Finally, there are plenty of gruesome masks, painted elephants and wooden toys on sale all over the island – and if you are in Colombo, be sure to bag a colourful cuddly animal or two from Barefoot *(see page 86)* before you leave.

FESTIVALS

It is sometimes said that Sri Lanka has more festivals than any other country in the world, and with 25 public holidays a year plus numerous festivals (lasting up to a month) from four different religions, it is easy to believe. The calendar on *page 98* gives only the most important of the country's innumerable shindigs. Virtually all the island's major festivals are religious in inspiration, and many centre around elaborate night-time processions, or *peraheras*, featuring lots of exquisitely dressed elephants, dancers and drummers. Many festivals occur on *poya* (full-moon) days, which are held to be sacred by Buddhists who traditionally retire to their temples to meditate and pray for the day. Most festivals follow the Buddhist lunar calendar, so dates vary slightly from year to year. For a complete listing of events and exact dates, visit <www.srilankatourism.org/events_festivals.asp>.

The Esala Perahera

Sri Lanka's most spectacular festival is the magnificent Esala Perahera, held in Kandy over the 10 days leading up to the Esala Poya in late July/early August (exact dates vary; check <www.srilankatourism.org/events_festivals.asp>). Held in honour of the city's revered Tooth Relic, the festival consists of a series of nightly processions around the city which gradually increase in scale and exuberance over the course of the 10 days. By the final few nights, the procession will have grown to mammoth proportions, with around a thousand dancers, drummers, fire-eaters and others, plus a hundred or so magnificently attired elephants, with a replica of the Tooth Relic carried on the back of the lead elephant, the so-called Maligawa Tusker – a vast explosion of noise, colour and religious pageantry without equal in Sri Lanka, or indeed anywhere else in Asia.

Festival Calendar

January *Duruthu Poya* commemorates the first of the Buddha's three legendary visits to the island with a spectacular procession at Kelaniya, just outside Colombo. On 14–15 January, the Hindu harvest festival of *Thai Pongol* is marked by ceremonies at Hindu temples across the island and the ceremonial cooking of newly garnered rice.

February *Navam Poya* is celebrated with a big elephant procession at Colombo's Gangaramaya temple – a relatively modern festival.

13–14 April The Buddhist and Hindu New Year (roughly coinciding with the west coast monsoon). Families swap gifts, *kiribath* (milk-cooked rice) cakes are eaten, new clothes worn and horoscopes cast.

Good Friday The island of Duwa hosts a major Easter Passion play

May The most important of Sri Lanka's poya days, *Vesak* combines a three-fold celebration of the Buddha's birth, enlightenment and death (all of which are traditionally believed to have occurred on this one day). Devout Buddhists visit their temple to meditate, free food is given out at the roadside and lamps are lit in front of houses.

June–August *Poson Poya*, the second most important of Sri Lanka's poya days, celebrates the introduction of Buddhism to the island by Mahinda, with pilgrims congregating on Anuradhapura and Mihintale.

July The lunar month of Esala is Sri Lanka's festival season. The most famous is Esala Perahera at Kandy *(see page 97)*, while there are also major festivals at Kataragama and Dondra.

August Honouring the god Skanda, *Vel* is one of the island's most important Hindu festivals, with colourful processions in Colombo during which the god's chariot is dragged across the city. Simultaneously, Jaffna celebrates the mammoth Nallur Festival, a 26-day festival dedicated to the same god and also featuring huge chariot processions, as well as gruesome acts of self-mutilation by devotees.

Late October/early November *Deepavali* is the Sri Lankan equivalent to North India's Diwali, celebrating the exploits of Rama and the triumph of good over evil.

25 December Christmas.

EATING OUT

Sri Lankan cooking is a lot like the island itself: a unique fusion of Indian, Asian and European influences which have been mixed together over the centuries to produce a highly flavoured and hugely enjoyable cuisine quite unlike any other. Rice and curry remains the national staple, though this plain name completely fails to describe the culinary magnificence of the best Sri Lankan cooking, while there are lots of intriguingly named local specialities to sample – *hoppers, string hoppers, lamprais, pittu, kottu rotty* and *watalappan*, to name just a few.

Central to the island's unique cuisine is its own distinctive local produce and its vast array of spices – Sri Lankan cooking is typically hot (and often downright fiery), with crisp chilli and coconut flavours which are often more reminiscent of Thai cooking than Indian. Adding to the heat are the distinctive local *sambols*, a kind of Sri Lankan salt and pepper, which are served as condiments – and you will probably come across the ubiquitous *pol sambol*, a bland-looking but palate-scorching combination of finely grated coconut and chilli. Approach with caution.

Curd stall, Konketiya

Tempting rice and curry spread

WHERE TO EAT

The main problem with Sri Lankan food is finding really good places to sample it: too many places, from the big west-coast resorts to smaller hotels and guesthouses around the island, offer up lame international tourist standards or tired buffets which give no hint of the island's wonderful cuisine – and, except in Colombo, decent independent restaurants are disappointingly thin on the ground. Having said that, there are a reasonable number of good places if you know where to look. A lot of the island's best restaurants are located in top-end hotels, some of which offer excellent cooking in luxurious surroundings. At the other end of the spectrum you will sometimes find excellent home cooking at relatively modest little guesthouses – a great opportunity for tourists to enjoy proper Sri Lankan home cooking at bargain prices.

Anywhere with even the slightest tourist pretensions will have an English-language menu – although wild variations in spelling can sometimes make it tricky to work out what is being offered. In the unlikely event that you end up eating in a local café you will just have to point at whatever food is on the counter or at what other diners are eating – though there will probably only be one or two choices available in any case.

WHAT TO EAT

Rice and Curry

Sri Lanka's national dish is rice and curry, a term which covers everything from the basic meals served up in local cafés to the sumptuous banquets dished up in the island's top hotels and restaurants. The classic Sri Lankan rice and curry features a dozen or more dishes of contrasting ingredients and flavours served with an enormous mound of rice – more akin to a South Indian thali (or even a Turkish

Breakfast and Snacks

Rolls are rather dry pancakes made from onion batter, eaten for breakfast with *sambol*, butter or marmalade, or as a snack. The traditional Sri Lankan breakfast consists of pancakes called *hoppers* (crispy on the outside, soft inside). If there is an egg in the middle, it will be an egg hopper. String hoppers are tangled circles of steamed noodles, which when eaten with a meat curry taste delicious, even in the morning. *Kiribeth* is a type of milk rice, usually served with *jaggery*, a sweetener made from palm syrup. For a snack, call in at a roadside stall and try a vegetarian spring roll or *cutlis*, pockets of dough filled with cold chicken or fish. Be warned: the meatballs and round, often fish-filled rolls *(malu pan)* are fiendishly hot. One dessert is *wattalappam*, a coconut crème caramel. Curd is a yoghurt made from buffalo milk – try it with *jaggery*.

meze or Indonesian *rijstafel*) than a traditional North Indian curry. The range of dishes varies from place to place but will usually feature a meat or fish curry, dhal and poppadums along with local favourites such as curried pineapple, caramelised aubergine, potato or sweet potato curry, curried green beans, *mallung* (shredded green vegetable fried with spices and coconut) and a range of *sambols*, as well as dishes using unusual local specialities such as drumsticks (a bit like okra), curried jakfruit or ash plantain. The range is pretty much endless, and part of the fun of travelling around the island is in sampling different local variations on the island's national dish.

Making *rotty*

Rice and curry is undoubtedly king in the Sri Lankan cookbook, but there are plenty of other local specialities worth sampling (see 'Breakfasts and Snacks' on *page 101*). *Lamprais* is a mound of rice plus toppings (typically a lump of chicken, a boiled egg and some pickle) baked and served in a banana leaf – a kind of simplified local take on the North Indian biriani.

The most popular Muslim contribution to Sri Lankan cooking is the *rotty*, a doughy pancake (similar to a Malaysian *murtabak*) wrapped up in various shapes around spicy dollops of vegetable or potato. Alternatively, *rotty* is chopped up and stir-fried with meat and vegetable to produce *kottu rotty*, a popular evening snack usually cooked on the spot outside local cafés by machete-wielding chefs –

So-called 'Maldive fish' (sun-dried tuna) is a popular ingredient in local cooking, adding a sharp, salty twist to curries and *sambols*.

listen for the noise of furious chopping and banging. You might also come across *pittu*, a mix of grated coconut and flour steamed in a cylindrical bamboo mould, and you will definitely find 'devilled' dishes (devilled pork, chicken and beef are all common) – bite-size hunks of meat served in a delicious, moderately-spicy barbecue sauce with big chunks of tomato, onion and chilli.

Seafood

Around the coast, seafood also plays a big role in the Sri Lankan diet, with a wide range of freshly caught fish – tuna, seer, mullet and shark among them – plus cuttlefish *(calamari)*, crab and prawns (those from the Negombo lagoon are particularly prized). Fiery fish curries are common, as is chilli crab, though otherwise preparation is fairly simple and usually not too spicy, with the fish grilled, bread crumbed or served in a simple garlic sauce.

International Cuisines

Other cuisines have also established themselves in the island's culinary mainstream. Colombo boasts dozens of excellent little South Indian restaurants, unpretentious places dishing up subcontinental classics like *dosas* (crispy rice pancakes), *iddlis* (steamed rice cakes) and *vadais* (spicy doughnuts made from deep-fried lentil-flour) at giveaway prices. Chinese food is also ubiquitous. Though generally spiced up for local tastes with distinctly un-Chinese hunks of chilli, it is often tasty and cheap. And in Colombo a lot of restaurants serve up the full range of international cuisine, from Japanese and Thai to Italian and French, with varying degrees of authenticity.

Desserts

Sri Lanka also has a good range of desserts. The classic pudding is *curd*, a deliciously thick and creamy yoghurt made from buffalo milk, usually served with honey. You might also encounter *wattalappam*, an egg-based dessert from Malaysia which tastes a bit like crème caramel. *Kiribath*, rice cooked in milk, is traditionally served at weddings and other festivals. More mainstream puddings and snacks include a decent range of ice-cream (the Elephant House brand is ubiquitous) and colourful cakes, often made in lurid colours and with a faintly curried flavour, are also popular, especially in Kandy. South Indian restaurants in Colombo usually have a selection of classic Indian sweets such as *laddu* and *burfi*.

Fruits

Sri Lanka also boasts a wonderful array of tropical fruits. Bananas come in all shapes and sizes, from fat little yellow miniatures to huge red monsters. Pineapple, mango and papaya are all found everywhere, as are coconuts. The enormous jakfruit, the world's biggest fruit, is often served curried as part of a rice and curry, while *durian*, another massive fruit, is a reputed aphrodisiac – though its peculiarly smelly aroma makes it something of an acquired taste. *Mangosteens* look like purple tomatoes and hold a delicious fruit which tastes like a slightly citrus-flavoured grape. The outlandish-looking *rambutan* is covered in bright red tentacles, inside which is a delicately flavoured, lychee-like fruit. Wood apples – round, apple-sized fruits covered in a tough

Tropical fruit

wooden shell – are also common; crack them open to discover a red, rather bitter seed-filled flesh, usually served softened with a dash of honey.

WHAT TO DRINK

Tea in Sri Lanka is a bit of a disappointment – most of the island's best stuff gets exported, meaning that you are unlikely to get more than a milky cup of tea-bag tea. There is also lots of locally grown coffee, which is usually quite palatable. International brands of fizzy drinks are available everywhere, though it is kinder to the local economy and your own teeth to stick to local brews. Ginger beer is a particular favourite, while there is also an interesting range of bizarre-tasting local fizzy pops to explore like Portello or Necta. Coconut milk is also available pretty much everywhere – look for men hanging around with a bunch of coconuts and a machete – and is claimed to be good for upset stomachs and hangovers alike thanks to its rich mix of glucose and potassium.

Sri Lankans love to booze, and the island isn't short of tipples both hard and soft. The nation's lager of choice is Lion Lager, followed by another local brew, Three Coins, and Carlsberg, brewed locally under licence. Imported wines are widely available at top-end hotels, though at a price, while a few bottles of rather strange-tasting Sri Lankan wines also occasionally make their way onto drinks lists. The island's top drink, however, is *arrack*, a feisty (33 percent proof) spirit made from refined toddy, tapped from coconut. Tasting a little like rum, *arrack* is available in various grades (double-distilled is easier on the palate and makes for softer hangovers). It can be drunk neat, mixed with coke or lemonade, or used as a base for all sorts of cocktails.

Stuffed *rotty* and tea for breakfast

To Help You Read the Menu...

ash plantain	Sri Lankan plantain, often used in curries
calamari	cuttlefish
dosa	crispy rice pancake
drumsticks	Sri Lankan vegetable, a bit like okra
hopper	small pancake served on its own or with various ingredients cooked inside
iddli	steamed rice cake
lamprais	rice plus toppings (chicken, egg and pickle) served in a banana leaf
mallung	shredded green vegetables fried with spices and coconut
kottu rotty	rotty chopped up and stir fried with meat and/or vegetables
pittu	a mix of grated coconut and flour steamed in a bamboo mould
rotty	a doughy pancake wrapped around spicy dollops of vegetable or potato
string hoppers	small roundels of fine rice noodles
sambols	spicy relishes served with curries
vadais	spicy doughnuts made from deep-fried lentil-flour

Desserts

curd	creamy yogurt made from buffalo milk
kiribath	rice cooked in milk
wattalappam	egg-based dessert, like creme caramel

Drinks

arrack	popular Sri-Lankan spirit, similar to rum and made from refined toddy
thambili	coconut milk
toddy	alcoholic drink made from coconut sap

HANDY TRAVEL TIPS

An A–Z Summary of Practical Information

A

ACCOMMODATION (see also CAMPING and RECOMMENDED HOTELS on page 128)

Sri Lanka has a vast range of accommodation in all price brackets, from ultra-basic $5-a-night guesthouses to luxurious $700-a-night boutique hotels and villas – the only common thread is that all are generally excellent value for money, and considerably cheaper than similar establishments in many other parts of Asia, let alone Europe or North America. Wherever there are tourists you will find accommodation, usually a surprisingly wide range, and the recent explosion in upmarket accommodation means that if you have got a bit of money, you can enjoy top-notch style and comforts at relatively affordable prices. Many of Sri Lanka's top hotels and guesthouses are almost attractions in their own right, and there is a plethora of romantic colonial-era properties and stylish modern hotels (exemplified by the island's superb string of Geoffrey Bawa-designed hotels, such as the Lighthouse and Kandalama – *see pages 132 and 136*) as well as more unusual offerings, whether you are looking for the chance to stay in a converted tea factory or a natural cave.

Simple guesthouses can be found all over the island, usually family-run affairs either in private houses or small-scale custom-built lodgings. Many offer excellent value for money, with comfortable rooms and good home cooking for $20 per night for a double, or often significantly less. Hotels come in all shapes and sizes, from simple business and tourist hotels ($30–50 a night), package tourist-oriented resort hotels ($50–100 a night) mainly found along the west coast, to five-star palaces in stunning modern or colonial properties (anything from $100 to $700 per night). There is also an ever-increasing number of luxury villas available for hire, usually lovingly restored colonial properties with bags of character – <www.villasinsrilanka.com> and <www.boutiquesrilanka.com> have the best selection.

Because of the large number of beds available it is almost never a problem finding a room, except at the very busiest times, though there is no harm in ringing or emailing ahead to reserve a room. The smaller and more exclusive the hotel, the more you are advised to book in advance, though it is usually fine to just turn up and take your chances at simple guesthouses. Prices in coastal areas fluctuate seasonally. Prices go up by anything from 10 to 50 percent during the season (November to April on the west coast; May to September on the east coast). Big festivals can also push prices through the roof, especially in Kandy during the Esala Perahera, or in Nuwara Eliya over Sinhalese New Year in April.

Note that there are no youth hostels in Sri Lanka.

AIRPORTS

Bandaranaike International Airport is located at Katunayake, 30km (19 miles) north of Colombo and 10km (6 miles) south of Negombo. There are plenty of unmetered taxis and touts hanging around: agree the fare in advance and count on around Rs.1,500 to Colombo (1hr), Rs.700 to Negombo (20min), or Rs.3,500 to Kandy (3hr). There are occasional buses to Colombo, but they are erratic and slow – not what you need after a long-haul flight.

The only other commercial airport is at Ratmalana, in the southern suburbs of Colombo near Mount Lavinia, from where three local operators run internal flights to Jaffna (at least three daily; 1hr) and Trincomalee (5 weekly; 1hr).

B

BICYCLE AND MOTORBIKE HIRE

The bicycle remains the staple form of transport for most Sri Lankans, and many guesthouses offer bikes for hire – anything from rusty old sit-up-and-beg antiques to state-of-the-art mountain bikes (from Rs.50–500 per day). If your guesthouse cannot help you, asking around the village or town where you are staying will usually turn up something.

Motorbike hire is also available in a number of coastal resorts – Negombo and Hikkaduwa both have a number of places renting out machines of various sizes, while you might also find bikes for hire elsewhere around the coast. Rates are generally very good value; a 250cc bike, for example, will usually cost around $10 per day.

BUDGETING FOR YOUR TRIP

Despite rampant inflation and significant price rises in recent years, Sri Lanka is still one of the cheaper countries in Asia to visit. How much you spend is really up to you: it is possible to scrape by on $10 a day by bedding down in a basic guesthouse and lolling on the beach. Equally, you could spend 50 times as much as this staying in the island's smartest hotels and availing yourself of the very best the island has to offer, including luxurious spa and ayurveda treatments and tours by balloon or private air taxi. As a rule of thumb, $50 per couple per day will get you acceptable accommodation and food and a reasonable range of tourist activities. For $100 per couple per day you can enjoy good mid- to upper-range accommodation and food and plenty of excursions. It is difficult to spend more than $200 per couple per day unless you stay in the very best hotels and splash out on lots of expensive activities

Transport on buses and trains is so cheap as to be almost free – you could travel from one end of the island to another for under $20. A car and driver will set you back $30–60 per day, depending on the quality of the vehicle and who you arrange it through. A filling meal can cost from $1 in a local cafe to $50 in a top restaurant, including drinks. The punitive fees levied on foreigners visiting government-run national parks ($30 and up once you have paid for transport) and archaeological sites ($20) can put a strain on budget travellers' finances, while Ayurveda and spa treatments cost anything from $20 to $200.

C

CAMPING

Accommodation in Sri Lanka is so cheap that there is no real reason to camp, and in any case the only officially recognised campsites are in the island's national parks. Ironically, camping in a national park (once you have factored in all the absurdly inflated fees which are levied on foreign visitors, plus the cost of transport and a driver) actually works out considerably more expensive than staying in even a mid-range hotel. If you are determined to experience a night under canvas in the wilds, various operators can fix you up with a guide, driver and all the necessary camping kit.

CAR HIRE (see also DRIVING)

This can work out quite cheap, with rates from as little as $30 per day, depending on the length of the hire period and the mileage to be covered, and is well worth it to avoid the stress of having to deal with public transport and make the most of your stay. As driving conditions can be poor, it is best to hire a car with a driver. This can be arranged pretty much anywhere on the island, either through a tour operator or through your guesthouse. Even places off the beaten track usually have local taxi drivers who will be happy to put themselves at your service for a day or for longer trips.

CLIMATE

Sri Lanka's climate is surprisingly complicated, with different weather patterns affecting different parts of the island. The welcome news is that there is always good weather in some part of the island at any time of year. The best time to visit the west and southwest coasts is from November to April; during the rest of the year the southwest (Yala) monsoon brings significant rainfall, with periodic deluges and overcast skies. The situation on the east coast is more or less exactly the opposite, the best time to visit being from

April to September; from October to February the northeast (Maha) monsoon brings considerable rain and unsettled conditions to this side of the island. The hill country receives rain from both monsoons, particularly the Yala monsoon, which dumps huge quantities of rain on the southwest side of the hills. As such, the best time to visit the hills is from January to April. The Cultural Triangle sees little rain, although sporadic downpours caused by the northeast monsoon may be experienced from October to December. Temperatures are fairly constant year round, and are determined by altitude rather than by season, averaging around 27°C (81°F) on the coast, 22°C (72°F) in Kandy and just 16°C (61°F) in Nuwara Eliya.

CLOTHING

As throughout South Asia, great importance is attached to personal appearance and cleanliness. Locals struggle to understand why visitors who can afford the airfare to Sri Lanka cannot also afford a decent set of clean clothes. Skimpy beachwear is fine on the beach, though it is best to cover up (women especially) away from the sand, and toplessness and naturism are not permitted anywhere. When visiting Buddhist (and most Hindu) temples you should remove shoes and hats and cover shoulders and legs.

CRIME AND SAFETY

For visitors, Sri Lanka is a reassuringly safe and law-abiding country. Petty theft and pickpocketing are much less widespread than in many Asian countries, while violent crimes against tourists are very uncommon. Nevertheless, it is wise to take sensible precautions and don't invite trouble by leaving hotel rooms unlocked or valuables lying around. Women should avoid walking on their own along dark beaches (or other places) at night.

The major safety concern in Sri Lanka is traffic. The island has one of the world's highest rates of road fatalities, and pedestrians are particularly at risk. Keep your eyes and ears peeled whenever there is traffic around, and never expect vehicles to stop (or even slow down) when you are crossing the road.

Another major safety issue is swimming *(see page 90)*. Never swim in an isolated spot on your own and always seek local advice if there is no-one else swimming off a particular section of beach (strong currents and undertows are common). Never go swimming under the influence of alcohol.

In the north and parts of the east, unexploded landmines are a potential hazard. Never go wandering off into uncleared areas in war-affected areas, even in built-up places – there are unexploded mines and ordnance even in the middle of Jaffna.

CUSTOMS AND ENTRY REQUIREMENTS

Citizens of the UK, Ireland, US, Canada, Australia, New Zealand and South Africa are given a free one-month tourist visa on arrival; this can easily be extended to three months at the Department of Immigration in Colombo (fees vary according to nationality).

When you leave Sri Lanka, you are not allowed to export any 'antiques' (classified as anything more than 50 years old) or any animal parts or marine products (including coral and shells) without a licence. If you need a licence, ask at the tourist office in Colombo for details.

D

DRIVING (see also CAR HIRE)

The anarchic driving conditions on Sri Lanka's roads and the cheapness of local labour mean that most visitors to the island end up hiring a car and driver for at least part of their stay.

If you are determined to drive yourself, a few operators offer self-drive car hire, though this can actually work out more expensive than going with a driver. Take your national driving licence (or, preferably, an international driving licence) and be sure to familiarise yourself with local driving conditions before getting behind the wheel yourself. Sri Lankan roads are no place for nervous drivers.

E

ELECTRICITY

Most sockets require round, three-pin plugs. The current is 220–240V 50 cycles AC. Adaptors for all sorts of foreign plugs are widely available in hardware, electronic and phone shops everywhere.

EMBASSIES, CONSULATES AND HIGH COMMISSIONS

Australia: 3 Cambridge Place, Colombo 7, tel: 011-269 8767.
Canada: 6 Gregory's Rd, Colombo 7, tel: 011-269 5841.
Republic of Ireland: Honorary Consul, 35 Edward Lane, Colombo 3, tel: 011-258 7895.
United Kingdom: 190 Galle Rd, Colombo 3, tel: 011-243 7336.
United States: 210 Galle Rd, Colombo 3, tel: 011-244 8007.

EMERGENCIES

There are no national emergency telephone numbers in Sri Lanka. In a medical emergency your guesthouse/hotel manager should be able to put you in touch with a local English-speaking doctor or send you to the nearest hospital.

G

GAY AND LESBIAN TRAVELLERS

Homosexuality is technically illegal in Sri Lanka, and although no-one has been convicted since the 1950s, the entire subject remains little understood and almost completely taboo. Discretion is advised. For information on the very secretive local scene, visit <www.geocities.com/srilankangay>. There are reviews of gay-friendly accommodation at <www.utopia-asia.com/tipssri.htm>.

GETTING THERE

The only way to reach Sri Lanka at present is by air – ferry services from India were discontinued at the beginning of the civil war in 1983 and are unlikely to resume for the foreseeable future. The island is well connected to international air networks. There are daily direct flights from London with SriLankan Airlines, and numerous one-stop routings, most conveniently via the Gulf with Emirates, Gulf Air, Qatar Airlines, Kuwait Airlines and Etihad, as well as via various European cities including Vienna, Zurich and Prague.

There are no direct flights to the island from Ireland, North America or Australasia. Travelling from Ireland or the east coast of the US and Canada there are numerous convenient one- or two-stop routings via London or other European or Gulf cities. From the west coast of the US and Canada there is a similarly wide range of one- or two-stop flights via Asian hubs including Tokyo, Hong Kong, Singapore, Bangkok, Kuala Lumpur and Jakarta.

Sri Lanka is well connected with many other Asian cities. SriLankan Airlines flies directly to 10 destinations in India, including Delhi and Mumbai, as well as to all the Asian hub cities listed above.

GUIDES AND TOURS

There are hundreds of tour agencies and guides around the country, of wildly varying standards. The following are the best established operators, often boasting a degree of local expertise and knowledge which easily surpasses that offered by foreign tour operators.

Adventure Sports Lanka 366/3 Rendapola Horagahakanda Lane, Talangama, Koswatta, Colombo, tel/fax: 011-279 1584, <www.actionlanka.com>. Sri Lanka's leading outdoor adventure specialists. Trips include kayaking and white-water rafting, mountain biking, canoeing and trekking.

Aitken Spence Travels 305 Vauxhall St, Colombo 2, tel: 011-230 8020, fax: 011-243 6382, <www.aitkenspencetravels.com>. General island tours, plus wildlife and nature tours through their eco-tourism arm, Nature Voyagers (<www.naturevoyagers.com>).

Colombus Tours 221–2 Dharmapala Mawatha, Colombo 7, tel: 011-269 7779, fax: 011-269 9371, <www.columbustours-srilanka.com>. Week-long tours with the emphasis on ecotourism, camping and trekking.

Jetwing Travels Jetwing House, 46/26 Navam Mawatha, Colombo 2, tel: 011-471 4830, fax: 011-234 5725, <www.jetwingtravels.com>. Solid island-wide tours run by Sri Lanka's largest hotel group.

Jetwing Eco-Holidays Jetwing House, 46/26 Navam Mawatha, Colombo 2, tel: 011-238 1201, fax: 011-471 4828, <www.jetwing eco.com>. Sri Lanka's premier eco-tourism operator, with an outstanding range of wildlife activities led by a team of expert guides.

Walkers Tours 130 Glennie St, Colombo 2, tel: 011-242 1101, fax: 011-243 9026, <www.walkerstours.com>. Reputable larger tour operators, offering general island-wide tours plus mountain-biking, trekking, bird watching, rafting, golf, watersports and diving packages.

H

HEALTH AND MEDICAL CARE

Immunisations are recommended for diphtheria, tetanus, hepatitis A and polio; you might also consider having yourself vaccinated for tuberculosis, meningitis and typhoid. Malaria is widespread except in the hills and parts of the west and south coasts – consult your doctor about which course of prophylaxis would work best for you. The most effective way of avoiding malaria is, of course, to avoid being bitten in the first place. Take plenty of mosquito repellent and cover up with light-coloured clothing from dusk onwards.

Although tap water in Sri Lanka is chlorinated and technically safe to drink, it is best to stick to bottled or boiled water since the unfamiliar micro-organisms contained by the local water may cause stomach upsets. Cases of mild diarrhoea caused by unsanitary food are much less common than in neighbouring India, but unfortunately a fair number of visitors do succumb. If you are unlucky enough to be struck down, drink lots of water to avoid dehydration and stick to bland foods like rice, yoghurt and bananas. Coconut milk is a good and safe source of liquid and contains valuable minerals such as potassium. If you have persistent severe diarrhoea, have a stool test to check for giardiasis and amoebic dysentery, both of which will require a course of antibiotics.

The tropical sun should not be underestimated. Remember that the effects of the sun are increased when reflected off water and sand, and that it is possible to burn even through cloud cover or when swimming. Always wear plenty of high-factor sun cream and cover up.

Standards of health care are reasonable; there are public hospitals in all major cities, plus numerous smaller private clinics. If you require treatment, the best first step is to ask at your hotel or guesthouse – any good establishment will be able to arrange for you to see an English-speaking doctor or to be taken to a reputable clinic.

HOLIDAYS

There are no fewer than 25 annual public holidays in Sri Lanka, plus many other festivals during which things grind to a halt. All 12 full-moon days (*poya* days) are Buddhist festivals and public holidays; these occur on the full-moon day of every month, and vary in exact date from year to year. The exact dates of the other public holidays marked with an asterisk below also vary from year to year; the dates given below are for 2006. The Muslim festivals listed below (and marked **) are timed according to local astronomical sightings of phases of the moon and again, the dates given below are for estimated dates in 2006, although these may vary slightly.

New Year's Day 1 January
Eid al-Adha** 10 January
Tamil Thai Pongal 14 January
Independence Day 4 February
Maha Sivarathri* 26 February
Milad un-Nabi 11 April
Sinhalese and Tamil New Year 13 and 14 April
Good Friday* 14 April
Labour Day 1 May
Deepavali 21 October
Eid al-Fitr** 22 October
Christmas Day 25 December
Eid al-Adha** 31 December

L

LANGUAGE

The main language is Sinhala, the language of the Sinhalese, spoken
by around 75 percent of the population. Tamil is the first language of
around 25 percent of the population, including not only the Tamils
themselves but also most east-coast Muslims. English is spoken pro-
ficiently by around 10 percent of the population (and less proficient-
ly by a far greater proportion), and serves as the major link language
between Tamils and Sinhalese, as well as being the language of business and tourism. Significant numbers of westernised Sri Lankans in
Colombo actually speak English as a first language alongside Sinhala. Anyone involved with tourism will almost certainly speak
good English, and you should have few problems communicating.
There is no practical incentive to learn any Sinhala except to satisfy
yourself. Sinhala speakers generally respond to foreigners' attempts
at speaking their language with incomprehension or, at best, polite
amusement. The following expressions will suffice to raise a grati-
fied smile, but for anything more complicated, stick to English.

hello/welcome/goodbye	**ayubowan**
yes	**oh-uh**
no	**nay**
please	**karuna karala**
thank you	**es-toothy**
sorry	**kana gartui**
excuse me	**sama venna**
What is your name?	**Nama mokada?**
My name is …	**Mahgah nama …**
How are you?	**Kohomada?**
Good, thanks.	**Honeen innava.**

M

MAPS

The best general map of the island is the Rough Guide map of Sri Lanka (1:500,000), which is extremely detailed, and also printed on indestructible plastic paper. The Nelles Sri Lanka map (1:450,000) is also good, if less durable and slightly less detailed. The Survey Department's *Road Atlas of Sri Lanka*, available from many bookshops in the island, has useful road maps and town plans.

MEDIA

Sri Lanka has plenty of English-language publications and radio stations. There are no fewer than five English-language national newspapers (three dailies and two Sunday papers). Three (*The Island*, *Daily News* and *Sunday Observer*) are indirectly controlled by the government, and so offer a rather biased view of events; better are the independently owned *The Daily Mirror* and *Sunday Times*, though the indifferent journalistic standards, curious style of written English and dense political jargon can make reading any of them a struggle. Foreign newspapers are only rarely available, and then at least a few days out of date; your best bet is to read them online. There is a burgeoning number of English-language monthly magazines as well. The excellent *Travel Sri Lanka* has insightful features on various aspects of the island, while *Travel Lanka* is also worth a look, as is the business-oriented *Lanka Monthly Digest*, which runs some good general-interest articles. In Colombo, *Leisure Times* has good listings of events in the capital and elsewhere.

A number of English-language radio stations broadcast out of Colombo (though reception away from the capital is patchy). These mainly serve up a fairly bland diet of Western pop and inane (if sometimes unintentionally comic) chat; the best is TNL Radio (101.7 FM). The BBC World Service and Voice of America are also widely broadcast. There is almost no locally produced English-language TV, though rooms in many smarter hotels have satellite TV offering the standard range of BBC, CNN and Star sports and movie channels.

MONEY

The Sri Lankan currency is the rupee, abbreviated variously as R, R/, or Rs. Coins come in denominations of Rs. 1, 2, 5 and 10, and 50 and 25 cents. Notes come in denominations of Rs.10, 20, 50, 100, 200 (rare), 500 and 1,000. At the time of writing the exchange rate was around Rs.180 to one British pound, and Rs.100 to one US dollar, although chronic inflation means that the value of the rupee is constantly depreciating. Change is usually in short supply except in more upmarket establishments – do not expect to pay for a Rs.50 rickshaw ride with a Rs.1000 note, and take the opportunity to break large notes wherever possible.

To guard against the effects of inflation, many smarter hotels and tour operators give prices in dollars or (increasingly) euros, although payment will be expected in rupees, calculated at the day's exchange rate. MasterCard and Visa are widely accepted at top-end places, and most towns around the island now have at least one ATM which accepts foreign MasterCard and Visa credit cards. Travellers' cheques are easily changed at any bank, although it is best to stick to cheques from a major brand (American Express and Thomas Cook are both safe bets) denominated in dollars, sterling or euros. Cash dollars, sterling and euros are also all easily exchanged at any bank, although exchanging other currencies might prove time-consuming.

O

OPENING TIMES

Government offices and larger businesses usually observe a standard five-day working week from Monday to Friday. Post offices usually open Mon–Sat 8am–6pm, or later at larger branches. Banks generally open Mon–Fri from around 8–9am to 2–3pm. Smaller businesses and shops tend to stay open seven days a week – there is no particular tradition of Sunday closures, although in Muslim areas businesses sometimes shut for all or part of Friday. Most restaurants are open daily from early in the morning until the last customer leaves, although some establishments in Colombo close in the afternoons from around 3–6pm. Some museums, especially those in Colombo, shut on Fridays, or on one other weekday. Buddhist temples tend to be open more or less around the clock; Hindu temples, by contrast, often stay shut between the early morning and late afternoon *pujas*.

P

POLICE

Sri Lankan police are generally friendly and will do their best to be helpful but are not noted for their English-language skills. If you have a problem or need to report a crime, it is best, if possible, to take a Sinhala-speaking local with you to assist with translation. There are tourist police offices in a few towns around the island, though they are usually no better than regular police stations.

POST OFFICES

There are post offices in all towns (and even some villages) across the island, usually open Mon–Sat from around 8am–6pm, or later. Those in larger towns have IDD phone and express mail (known locally as EMS Speed Post) services, as well as free poste restante facilities (ask for mail to be addressed 'c/o The Postmaster, General Post Office, Town' with your surname underlined). If sending a parcel abroad, take the contents unwrapped to the post office for inspection before you wrap them up – larger post offices usually have kiosks selling string, tape and brown paper.

PUBLIC TRANSPORT

Public transport is plentiful and incredibly cheap, but also generally slow and uncomfortable.

Bus. The staple means of transport is by bus; every town of any size on the island has regular services, and there are very few places where the network doesn't reach. Buses are either of two types. Government-run buses (usually big orange rustbuckets) are the cheapest, slowest and most crowded, and tend to stop everywhere and anywhere there is a passenger to be picked up. Private buses come in all sorts of forms: the most basic resemble government-run buses in speed and (lack of) comfort. Faster services (usually signed 'semi-express' or 'express') tend to make more limited stops and to be a bit quicker, at least in theory. Fastest of all are the privately run express minibuses which ply the routes between major cities. These are often twice as fast as the other buses; the interiors are rather cramped, but at least they don't usually get clogged up with standing passengers, as the slower and larger buses do. Fares on all buses are extremely cheap, ranging from as little as Rs.20 per hour of travel on the cheapest buses up to Rs.70 per hour on express minibuses. Advance reservations are virtually unheard of, except on Colombo–Jaffna buses. All larger towns have bus terminals, though it is often possible to flag down buses by the roadside.

Train. The island's extensive railway network is a legacy of the British colonial period, and has been little changed since. Trains are as slow as, or even slower than, buses, and delays and over-crowding are the norm. Nevertheless, for many visitors the system's shabby, old-fashioned charm has an undeniable attraction, best experienced by a ride on the scenic hill country line from Colombo to Kandy and beyond to Nuwara Eliya and Badulla – one of the most beautiful lines in Asia. Fares are dirt cheap – the standard (second-class) fare from Colombo to Kandy, for example, costs less than a dollar. Most trains consist of basic second- and even more basic third-class carriages; seats in these carriages cannot be reserved, so the chances are that you might end up standing for at least part of the ride. The hill country train also has a so-called 'observation carriage', with large windows and plusher than usual seating. Places in the observation carriage have to be reserved in advance (most easily done at Colombo Fort or Kandy stations) and tend to sell out quickly, so you will have to be particularly well organised or lucky to bag a seat.

Tuktuk. The Sri Lankan rickshaw, known variously as tuktuks, three-wheelers or (somewhat euphemistically) 'taxis', are the staple means of covering short distances around towns, and can sometimes be useful for covering longer journeys in the country in places where bus services are sketchy. Bargaining is the order of the day, and you should always agree a fare before setting off to avoid arguments, unpleasantness and rip-offs later. Estimating how much a journey should cost is difficult, but as a rough rule of thumb count on Rs.30–40 per kilometre. The longer the journey, the cheaper the per-kilometre rate should be.

Plane. There are regular domestic services from Colombo's Ratmalana airport to Jaffna and Trincomalee; both flights take about an hour and, at a cost of around $120 return, make an attractive alternative to the eight- to twelve-hour overland journeys. SriLankan Airlines also runs an air taxi service from Colombo to various places around the country using water planes which land either in the sea or in local lakes. Flights offer a scenic and extremely convenient way of getting around, although most services operate only on demand and don't come cheap. Seats cost $100–400 with a minimum of four passengers per flight. See <www.srilankan.aero> for details.

R

RELIGION

The world's four largest religions are all practised in Sri Lanka. The majority of the population (about 70 percent) are Buddhist, while the remainder is more or less equally divided between Hindus, Muslims and Christians. Almost all Sinhalese are Buddhist, while most Tamils are Hindu (though there are also significant numbers of Tamil Christians). The island's Muslims are all descendants of traders or immigrants from Arabia, India, Malaysia and Indonesia. Religion remains a dominant cultural force throughout the island in all communities.

T

TELEPHONE

The country code for Sri Lanka is 94; the international access code to dial out of Sri Lanka is 00, followed by the relevant country code. All Sri Lankan landline numbers now have 10 digits, including a three-digit area code. There are few public phone booths on the street in Sri Lanka; it is usually easier to find a 'communications bureau' – there are usually a least a couple of these in any town of note, offering phone, fax and sometimes email facilities, along with photocopying and mobile-phone accessories. You make your call either from a phone booth or from a phone at the counter and pay the bill at the end: count on around Rs.150 per minute for calls to the UK, North America and Australasia. Most smarter hotels have in-room IDD phones, but rates from these are significantly higher. Local and national calls don't usually cost more than about Rs.10 per minute.

There is good mobile coverage across most parts of the island, even in the north; ask your phone company if you want to use your mobile. Alternatively, you can buy a Sri Lankan SIM card for around $20 which gets you a local phone number and allows you to make international calls for as little as Rs.30 per minute; Dialog and Celltel are the two largest companies.

TIME DIFFERENCES

Sri Lankan time is six hours ahead of Greenwich Mean Time.

TIPPING AND TAXES

The upmarket hotels and restaurants often add a service charge of 10 percent to their bills, and you might also be hit with a 15 percent GST (Government Service Tax). The resultant 25 percent surcharge on top of published prices can be a nasty surprise when you come to pay the bill, so it is always worth checking menus and hotel rates when you arrive. More downmarket establishments rarely levy either charge. If you think you have been well looked after, a tip of 10 percent or so should suffice.

TOILETS

There are no public toilets in Sri Lanka, although as a foreigner you should not have any problems wandering into the nearest hotel to discreetly avail yourself of the facilities. Almost all toilets are Western-style flush toilets rather than Asian squat toilets, and are usually kept tolerably clean. Toilet paper is almost always provided, though there's no harm in carrying some emergency supplies.

TOURIST INFORMATION

Official sources of tourist information in Sri Lanka are virtually non-existent. There are only two properly set-up tourist information of-

fices, in Colombo (80 Galle Road, Colombo 3, tel: 011-243 7055) and
Kandy (Temple Street, by the entrance to the Temple of the Tooth, tel:
081 222 2661). This massive gap is filled by local guesthouse owners
and local tour operators. Many guesthouse owners are experts in their
area and can tell you all you need to know, as well as arranging car
hire, tours and other services. Tour operators can also be found all
over the island, especially in Colombo and down the west coast, and
can often be valuable sources of information and practical help.

Sri Lanka Tourism has several offices around the world:
Australia: 29 Lonsdale St, Braddon, ACT 2612, tel: 02-6230 6002,
fax: 6230 6066.
Ireland: 59 Ranelagh Rd, Dublin 6, tel: 01-496-9621,
fax: 01-496 5345.
UK: Clareville House, 26–27 Oxendon St, London SW1Y 4EL,
tel: 0207-930 2627, email: srilankatourism@aol.com.
US: 115 Inner Ave, 323 Edison, NJ 08820, tel: 732-516 9800,
fax: 732 452-0087, email:<ctbUSA@anlusa.com>.

W

WEBSITES AND INTERNET CAFÉS

The Sri Lanka Tourist Board website at <www.srilankatourism.org>
has a decent range of basic information, and it's also worth visiting
the excellent <www.travelsrilanka.com>. For news, visit <www.
bbc.co.uk/news> and enter 'Sri Lanka' in the search box to bring up
a huge archive of stories. <www.bbc.co.uk/sinhala> is also a good
source of breaking news. Colombo and Kandy have plenty of well-
set up internet cafés with broadband connections, whereas many
more remote places remain obdurately offline. In general, however,
anywhere which sees a reasonable number of tourists is likely to
have places offering internet access, and most top-end hotels also
have access. Rates vary from Rs.1 per minute in Colombo and
Kandy up to Rs.10 per minute in less busy places.

Recommended Hotels

Sri Lanka boasts a plethora of accommodation in all price ranges, and the following listings represent only a small selection of the very best of what's available. Reservations are pretty much essential at the more upmarket places, while the better budget guesthouses can also get booked up at busy times of the year, so it's always worth phoning a couple of days in advance to make sure of a room. Prices in most places vary according to season and demand; establishments along the west and (to a lesser extent) south coasts generally hike their prices up from November through to April. Rates at many places can be negotiable, especially if business is slow and you're planning on staying for a few days. Rooms in more expensive establishments are usually quoted in dollars, though they are payable in rupees at the daily exchange rate. Many more upmarket places levy a 10 percent service charge and a 15 percent government service tax on top of the basic room rate, adding a nasty twist to the final bill if you're not expecting it.

As a basic guide to prices, we have used the following symbols (for a standard double or twin room in high season):

$$$$$	over $200
$$$$	$100–200
$$$	$50–100
$$	$25–50
$	below $25

COLOMBO

Galle Face Hotel $$$ *Galle Face Green, Colombo 3, tel: 011-254 1010, fax: 011-254 1072, <www.gallefacehotel.com>.* Famous old colonial hotel and Colombo landmark, with lots of period charm and an unrivalled oceanfront setting at the south end of Galle Face Green. Rooms in the old ('Classic') wing are somewhat faded, though they retain a certain old-fashioned aura, while those in the new Regency Wing offer colonial style combined with modern international-standard luxury. There is also an attractive new spa and a romantic seafront bar and restaurant.

Havelock Place Bungalow $$$$ *6 Havelock Place, Colombo 5, tel: 011-258 5191, <www.bungalow.lk>.* Colombo's only boutique hotel, this peaceful, low-key hideaway is tucked away in the southern city in a pair of stylishly converted colonial bungalows which combine period character and modern comforts.

Hilton $$$$$ *2 Sir Chittampalam A Gardiner Mawatha, Colombo 2, tel: 011-249 2492, fax: 011-254 4657, <www.hilton.com>.* One of the smartest in Colombo, this slick modern five-star hotel has comfortable, if smallish, rooms with ocean views and plenty of facilities, including a string of excellent restaurants and the city's best nightclub.

Mount Lavinia Hotel $$$$ *Hotel Road, Mount Lavinia, tel: 011-271 5221, fax: 011-273 8228, <www.mountlaviniahotel.com>.* Sprawling landmark hotel set on the seafront in the beachside suburb of Mount Lavinia. Built around the 19th-century residence of former British governor Sir Thomas Maitland, the hotel combines period atmosphere with contemporary comforts. There is also a gorgeous stretch of private beach, an excellent spa and one of Mount Lavinia's best restaurants. Very popular with foreign wedding parties and honeymooners.

THE WEST COAST

BERUWALA, ALUTHGAMA AND BENTOTA

Club Villa $$$ *138/15 Galle Road, Bentota, tel: 034-227 5312, fax: 034-428 7129, <www.club-villa.com>.* One of the most personable small hotels in Sri Lanka, set in a beautiful spot at the quiet southern end of Bentota beach and occupying a scatter of intimate, superbly designed colonial-style buildings set around a gorgeous garden running down to the sea.

Hemadan $ *25 River Avenue, Aluthgama, tel: 034-227 5320, email: <hemadan@wow.lk>.* The most characterful accommodation in Aluthgama, this appealing little guesthouse has simple but comfortable rooms in a pleasant white building with an attractive little garden running down to the Bentota lagoon – a beautiful spot. There is a free boat service over to the quiet stretch of beach opposite if you want to get out onto the sand.

Neptune $$$$ *Moragalla, Beruwala, tel: 034-227 6031, fax: 034-227 6033, <www.aitkenspencehotels.com>.* The most stylish of the numerous large resorts which clutter the main section of Beruwala beach, with bright and comfortable rooms in an elegant modern building whose sweeping wings enclose an attractive pool and extensive gardens.

Saman Villas $$$$$ *Aturuwella, Bentota, tel: 034-227 5435, fax: 034-227 5433, <www.samanvilla.com>.* Stunningly situated on a bluff high above the ocean with sweeping views up and down the coast, this ultra-chic boutique hotel has luxurious rooms filled with every conceivable mod-con, a gorgeous spa and one of the most spectacular swimming pools in Sri Lanka.

Serendib Hotel $$$ *Bentota, tel: 034-227 5353, fax: 034-227 5313, <www.serendibleisure.com>.* Unpretentious but quietly stylish beachfront resort hotel on one of the nicest stretches of beach in Bentota. Rooms are simple but good value, and the whole atmosphere is pleasantly low-key compared with other nearby resorts – and there is a beautiful new spa to dive into if you need to unwind.

Tropical Gardens $$$ *Moragalla, Beruwala, tel: 034-227 6157, fax: 034-227 6156, <www.jetwing.net>.* This hugely original and cunningly designed four-star hotel is a five-minute walk from the seafront. The attractive low-rise buildings completely enclose a gorgeous rectangle of tropical garden (hence the name) stuffed full of lush evergreen trees and abundant bird life – an intimate and captivating oasis, and far nicer than the tout-plagued beach itself.

HIKKADUWA

Amaya Reef $$$ *400 Galle Road, tel: 091-438 3244, fax: 091-438 3243, <www.amayaresorts.com>*. Hikkaduwa's only top-end hotel (though at a very reasonable price), this attractive new beachfront establishment encapsulates all that is best about contemporary Sri Lankan design, with beautiful minimalist rooms in muted shades of teak, ochre and white, and a good open-air seafront restaurant.

Neela's $ *634 Galle Road, Narigama, tel: 091-227 5312, email: <neelas_sl@hotmail.com>*. This long-established guesthouse is one of the friendliest and best-value places to stay in Hikkaduwa, with a fine beachside location, good home-cooking and bright and comfortable modern rooms.

NEGOMBO

The Beach $$$$$ *Porutota Road, Negombo, tel: 031-227 3500, fax: 031-227 3555, <www.jetwing.net>*. This is Negombo's only five-star hotel, with stylish and superbly appointed rooms, excellent food, a pleasant beachfront setting at the quiet north end of the beach and a beautiful pool, part of which winds underneath the hotel itself between strategically placed frangipani trees.

Browns Beach Hotel $$$ *Lewis Place, tel: 031-487 0573, fax: 031-487 0572, <www.aitkenspenceholidays.com>*. Large and attractive resort hotel which rambles for a considerable distance along the beach, but manages to feel cheerful and surprisingly homely despite its size. Rooms are unpretentious (those in the main building are better value than the beach bungalows) and there is a huge pool and plenty of other facilities.

Silver Sands $ *Lewis Place, tel: 031-222 2880, <www.silversands.go2lk.com>*. This attractive budget beachside hotel is one of Negombo's longest-running cheapies, and remains one of the most popular thanks to its comfortable and excellent-value rooms. It has a pleasant restaurant, courtyard garden, and friendly family atmosphere.

THE SOUTH

GALLE

Amangalla $$$$$ *10 Church Street, tel: 091-223 3388, fax: 091-223 3355, <www.amanresorts.com>.* Occupying the sensitively restored premises of Galle's famous old New Oriental Hotel, this establishment remains wonderfully faithful to the period character of its colonial predecessor, combining old-world colonial chic with the last word in contemporary luxury – a compelling combination, though it is not cheap.

Beach Haven $ *65 Lighthouse Street, tel: 091-223 4663, email: <thalith@sri.lanka.net>.* This perennially popular guesthouse seems to have been going for ever and continues to pull in visitors thanks to its cheap and comfortable rooms, tasty home cooking and its uniquely friendly and sociable family atmosphere.

Galle Fort Hotel $$$$$ *28 Church Street, tel: 091-223 2870, fax: 091-223 2939, <www.galleforthotel.com>.* Stunning new hotel set in a magnificently converted old Dutch warehouse – like the nearby Amangalla, it manages to combine colonial charm and contemporary luxury, though at a far more affordable price. It also dishes up some of Sri Lanka's best foreign cuisine, with a predominantly Southeast Asian slant – a pleasant change if you have had one too many rice and curries.

The Lighthouse $$$$$ *Dadella, tel: 091-222 4017, fax: 091-222 4021, <www.jetwing.net>.* Set on a breezy stretch of seafront a couple of kilometres outside Galle, this Geoffrey Bawa-designed hotel is one of the great Sri Lankan architect's defining creations, with a simple, serene exterior, gorgeously designed rooms and splashes of local colour (such as the remarkable wrought-iron staircase depicting the Portuguese arrival in Sri Lanka). Excellent food and heaps of facilities too.

The Sun House $$$$ *18 Upper Dickson Road, tel: 091-438 0275, <www.thesunhouse.com>.* This long-established boutique guesthouse is still one of the nicest places to stay in Sri Lanka, set in a beautiful old 19th-century planter's villa on a hill high above Galle which has oodles of period charm as well as memorable cooking. The adjacent Dutch House offers a slightly more upmarket variation on the same theme, with four huge suites in another historic colonial mansion.

UNAWATUNA

Thaproban $$ *Unawatuna Village, tel: 091-438 1722.* Poking up from the centre of Unawatuna like an eccentric orange lighthouse, this unusual-looking hotel has bright and cheery (if slightly small) rooms right above the beach, and one of the village's best restaurants.

Thambapanni Retreat $$$ *Unawatuna Village, tel: 091-223 4588, fax: 091-223 3130, email: <thambapanni@sltnet.lk>.* Set a few minutes' walk from the beach, up against the lush, jungle-covered flanks of Rumassala (the huge rocky outcrop behind Unawatuna village), this place has more the atmosphere of a rainforest eco-lodge than a beach hotel. Rooms are comfortable, with neo-colonial furnishings and all mod-cons, and there is a small pool.

TANGALLA

Amanwella $$$$$ *Godelluwela, Tangalla, tel: 047-224 1333, fax: 047-224 1334, <www.amanresorts.com>.* Set on one of the south's most beautiful and unspoilt beaches, this sublime new hotel offers the finest beachfront accommodation anywhere on the island. Rooms are sumptuous little masterpieces of chic modern interior design, and the overall concept is a serenely simple and artfully understated exercise in low-impact contemporary architecture, whose minimalist lines merge gracefully with the wonderful natural setting. The only disappointment is the huge price tag attached.

KANDY

Helga's Folly $$$$ *Off Mahamaya Mawatha, tel: 081-447 4314, fax: 081-447 9370, <www.helgasfolly.com>.* Sri Lanka's most eccentric hotel, set on a hill high above Kandy. The interior is like a kind of mad museum, with brightly coloured rooms stuffed with huge quantities of bric a brac – animal heads, colonial photos, Indonesian puppets and huge candles covered in clumps of dripping wax – while all rooms are individually decorated with colourful murals. The relative paucity of facilities (apart from a very shallow swimming pool) – and package tourists – is all part of the allure.

Hotel Suisse $$$ *30 Sangaraja Mawatha, tel: 081-222 2637, fax: 081-223 2083, <www.ccom.lk/suisse>.* Long-established lakeside hotel (Mountbatten had his wartime headquarters here) with spacious and very comfortable rooms and a quietly understated old-fashioned character, including a cosy bar and a fine billiards room.

Hunas Falls $$$ *Elkaduwa, 27km north of Kandy, tel: 081-247 6402, fax: 071-273 5134, <www.jetwing.net>.* Located 27km (17 miles) north of Kandy in the village of Elkaduwa, up in the rugged hills of the Knuckles range, this eco-oriented retreat is the nicest of the many hotels around Kandy, with comfortable modern facilities, a stunning setting and plenty of walks and wildlife in the surrounding countryside.

Sharon Inn $ *59 Saranankara Road, tel/fax: 081-222 5665, <www.hotelsharoninn.com>.* Neat, modern and very professionally run guesthouse with comfortable rooms, excellent food and superb views over the lake and town from its hillside setting.

THE HILL COUNTRY

ELLA AND BANDARAWELA

Ambiente $ *2km (1 mile) from Ella Village, tel: 057-222 8867.* This low-key modern guesthouse is in one of the best locations in Sri Lanka, high on a hilltop above Ella village with superb views over Ella Gap. Rooms are comfortable, if on the small side, and the food is good, too.

Bandarawela Hotel $$$ *14 Welimada Road, tel: 057-222 2501, fax: 057-222 2834, <www.aitkenspencehotels.com>*. Atmospheric colonial-style hotel set in a 19th-century planters' club house. The rambling old wooden building is full of character, and rooms have bags of old-world ambience – all at a very reasonable price.

Ravana Heights $$ *Wellawaya Road, Ella Village, tel: 057-222 8888, <http://ravanaheights.com>*. This attractive, small modern guesthouse has bright, comfortable rooms and unforgettable views of Ella Gap through its big picture windows. There is also excellent home cooking, and the friendly owner can even sometimes be persuaded to escort guests on hikes through the surrounding countryside.

NUWARA ELIYA

Glendower $$ *Grand Hotel Road, tel: 052-222 2501, fax: 052 222 2749, e-mail: <hotel_glendower@hotmail.com>*. This modest little half-timbered hotel is Nuwara Eliya's cosiest mid-range option, with period touches, attractive wood-floored rooms, a pub-style bar and the excellent *King Prawn* Chinese restaurant *(see page 142)*.

The Hill Club $$$ *Off Grand Hotel Road, tel: 052-222 2653, fax: 052-222 2654, email: <hillclub@eureka.lk>*. Set in a rugged old granite and half-timbered building close to the town centre, this famous old hotel offers a real taste of colonial Ceylon. The time-warped interior includes a musty billiards room, men-only bar and an atmospheric restaurant, plus assorted stuffed stags' heads, cracked leather furniture and shelves of yellowing novels. Accommodation is in neat, slightly chintzy rooms with creaking wooden floors – like a rather superior British B&B.

St Andrews $$$$ *10 St Andrew's Drive, tel: 052-222 3031, fax: 052 222 3153, <www.jetwing.net>*. Nuwara Eliya's smartest hotel, occupying a beautiful colonial country club surrounded by graceful lawns running down to the golf course. The oak-panelled bar and restaurant are pure Edwardian period pieces, while rooms are cosy and comfortable.

Tea Factory $$$$ *Kandapola, tel 052-222 9526, fax: 052-222 9606, <www.aitkenspencehotels.com>.* Stunning hotel set in an ingeniously converted tea factory – the factory exterior has been perfectly preserved, but the interior has been magically transformed into a sleek modern hotel. Five-star comforts and a stylish design that combines futuristic architectural lines with lots of old tea-making memorabilia and machines. The setting is another huge attraction, high up in one of the most spectacular parts of the Nuwara Eliya region and surrounded by miles of tea plantation – ask the resident naturalist to show you around.

THE CULTURAL TRIANGLE

ANURADHAPURA

Tissawewa Rest House $$ *Old Town, tel: 025-222 2299, fax: 025-222 3265, <www.quickshaws.com>.* This marvellously atmospheric old colonial rest house has a great period charm and an unbeatable location right at the heart of the old ruined city – the only place to stay in Anuradhapura actually inside the Sacred Precinct (though this also means that no alcohol is served). Not the plushest place to stay in town, but easily the most memorable.

DAMBULLA

Kandalama $$$$ *Kandalama Lake, 10km (6 miles) from Dambulla, tel: 066-228 4100, fax: 066-228 4109, <www.aitken spencehotels.com>.* One of Sri Lanka's most famous hotels, this hugely original Bawa-designed establishment offers the ultimate union of architecture and nature, clinging as it does to the underside of a huge rocky outcrop and almost completely buried by layers of tropical vegetation so that, despite its considerable size, from certain angles it is almost invisible. Stunning views of Sigiriya and the

Kandalama lake, neatly equipped and very reasonably priced rooms, and one of the island's most spectacular swimming pools all add to the allure.

HABARANA

The Lodge $$$$ *Habarana Village, tel: 066-227 0011, fax: 011-537 3304, <www.johnkeellshotels.com>*. Located in the crossroads town of Habarana, and conveniently placed for day trips to all the Cultural Triangle's major sites (if you bring your own car), this rustic, low-key hotel has plush accommodation in individual villas scattered around extensive and beautiful tree-shaded grounds.

POLONNARUWA

Rest House $$ *Polonnaruwa, tel: 027-222 2299*. Perched on the edge of the great Parakrama Samudra lake, and close to the ancient city, this beautiful yet simple and homely old rest house has a certain old-fashioned charm. Queen Elizabeth II stayed here in 1954, and it looks as if not much has changed since.

THE EAST COAST

TRINCOMALEE

Nilaveli Beach Hotel $$$ *Nilaveli, tel: 026-223 2295, fax: 026-223 2297, <www.tangerinehotels.com>*. Unpretentious, long-established resort hotel right on Nilaveli beach opposite Pigeon Island, with a range of comfortable rooms of varying prices and standards and a decent range of facilities.

ARUGAM BAY

Hideaway $ *Arugam Bay, tel: 063-224 8259*. Attractive and excellent-value small guesthouse set a few minutes inland from the beach. Rooms are simple but attractively furnished, while the owner's striking photos of elephants from nearby Lahugala National Park decorate the corridors and verandah.

Recommended Restaurants

Outside Colombo, there are relatively few independent restaurants; you'll probably eat in your hotel or guesthouse, virtually all of which offer food of some sort, ranging from bland international-style buffets to excellent traditional home cooking. Hotel and guesthouse restaurants open for breakfast from around 8am and stay open for the rest of the day and evening. Restaurants in Colombo often close in the afternoons from around 3pm to 6pm, and a few open only in the evenings.

Eating in Sri Lanka is usually very good value. Even in the smartest restaurants and hotels you'll usually find things on the menu for under $10 (although the most expensive seafood dishes can cost double this), while in cheap local cafés you can still get a filling meal for around a dollar. It's not usually necessary to book in advance. Only the smarter hotels and restaurants accept credit cards; everywhere else you'll need to have cash. The price codes below refer to the average price of a main course for one person.

$$$	over $8
$$	$4–8
$	below $4

COLOMBO

Barefoot Cafe $ *706 Galle Road, Colombo 3, tel: 011-258 0114.* Set in the beautiful courtyard at the back of Colombo's finest shop, this little urban oasis offers unpretentious but well-prepared café-standards including sandwiches, pasta dishes and good daily specials, as well as juices, milkshakes and moreish puddings. Daily until 7pm.

Chesa Swiss $$$ *3 Deal Place, Colombo 3, tel: 011-257 3433.* Swiss-owned restaurant in a lovely colonial villa whose consistently good food draws a faithful expat clientele. Classic Swiss dishes (fondues, rosti, barley soup) share menu space with prime Australian steaks, seafood and vegetarian dishes. Only open in the evening.

Cricket Club Cafe $$ *34 Queens Road, Colombo 3, tel: 011-250 1384.* One of Colombo's most popular eating and drinking haunts, this cricket-themed café has walls plastered with photos, scorecards and signed bats, and a simple but tasty selection of burgers, stir fries, steaks and daily specials. The cosy little pub-style bar gets lively with expats and tourists after dark.

Curry Leaf $$$ *Hilton Hotel, 2 Sir Chittampalam A. Gardiner Mawatha, Colombo 2, tel: 011-249 2492.* The jungle village decor at this outdoor restaurant may be a bit cheesy, but the nightly Sri Lankan buffet is one of the city's best places to introduce yourself to the island's culinary delights, from string hoppers to *wattalapan*, plus oodles of rice and curry. Only open in the evening.

Gallery Café $$ *2 Alfred House Road, Colombo 3, tel: 011-258 2162.* This ultra-chic courtyard cafe is set in a wonderfully stylish building designed by Geoffrey Bawa, who used to have his office here. There is decent food from an international menu, or just go for a coffee and the chance to rub shoulders with Colombo's smart set.

Greenlands $ *Shrubbery Gardens, Colombo 4.* A Colombo institution, this perennially popular restaurant serves up generous portions of top-notch South Indian vegetarian cooking at giveaway prices. The menu features *dosas*, *iddlis* and *vadais* galore, and if you've still got room afterwards there is a huge glass cabinet filled with colourful South Indian sweets at the entrance.

Royal Thai $$$ *Trans Asia Hotel, 115 Sir Chittampalam A. Gardiner Mawatha, Colombo 2, tel: 011-249 1000.* An intimate Thai restaurant with sumptuous oriental decor. The menu features both mainstream dishes like *pad thai* and *tom yam*, and more unusual offerings.

THE WEST COAST

Bijou $$ *44 Porutota Road, Negombo, tel: 031-531 9577.* Swiss-owned restaurant with a homely pine interior and an excellently prepared selection of Swiss and central European dishes (fondues, steaks and so on), as well as some of the best seafood in Negombo.

Firefly $$$ *364 Galle Road, Dodonaduwa, 4km (3 miles) south of Hikkaduwa.* Occupying a superbly restored colonial villa, this chic new restaurant offers tempting fusion cuisine prepared by its New York owner-cum-head chef and making ample use of fresh local produce, especially seafood.

Lords $$$ *Porutota Road, Negombo.* Sleek modern bar-restaurant with stylish decor and a beautifully presented selection of international cuisine ranging from fish and chips to more unusual offerings like cashew nut and raisin curry.

Refresh $$ *384 Galle Road, Hikkaduwa, tel: 091-227 7810.* One of the best independent restaurants on the west coast, with perhaps the fattest menu on the island, featuring a staggering array of local and international cuisine. It is the only place on the island you will find *gazpacho, gado-gado* and *falafel* all under one roof, and they also do a lavish rice and curry spread, as well as all sorts of interesting Sri Lankan breakfasts.

Sands $$$ *The Beach Hotel, Negombo, tel: 031-227 3500.* The beachside restaurant at Negombo's top hotel provides a romantic setting for a range of excellently prepared international dishes, including one of the west coast's best rice and curry spreads.

THE SOUTH COAST

Galle Fort Hotel $$$ *28 Church Street, Galle Fort, tel: 091-223 2870.* The food at this stunning new hotel is some of the best non-Sri Lankan cooking you will find on the island, with the emphasis on fresh seafood and light, delicately flavoured Australian-style Southeast Asian food. Try either the lavish evening set menus

($20–30 for anything up to nine courses) or the more casual lunch and snack menu. Or just sit down with a coffee on the beautiful street-facing veranda.

Khaled's $$ *102 Pedlar Street, Galle Fort, Galle, tel: 091-223 4907.* This simple little Galle guesthouse has been garnering rave reviews for many years for the excellent home cooking prepared by Mrs Khaled, especially her tempting rice and curry spread. Nonguests are welcome, though it is a good idea to give them a few hours' notice.

Refresh $$ *Kataragama Road, Tissamaharama, tel: 047-223 7357.* This is a Tissamaharama offshoot of the well-known Hikkaduwa original. The menu is only about a third the size of the Hikkaduwa branch, but the food is uniformly excellent, with a decent range of seafood and Sri Lankan standards.

The Sun House $$$ *18 Upper Dickson Road, tel: 091-438 0275.* Even if you are not staying here, it's worth the walk up the hill for an evening meal at this superb little boutique hotel. The setting in an old colonial villa is incomparably romantic, and the food, featuring a daily-changing set menu of three-course dinners showcasing the very best of Sri Lankan and Indian Ocean cuisine is likely to be amongst the very best you will find on the island. Book before 1pm for dinner.

KANDY

Devon Restaurant $ *11 Daladu Vidiya.* The decor at this functional modern restaurant won't win any awards but the food is cheap, tasty and unpretentious. Choose from an extensive menu featuring *burianis, lamprais*, noodles, devilled dishes and lots more, as well as tasty hoppers for breakfast.

Flower Song $ *137 Kotugodella Vidiya, tel: 081-222 3628.* There's not much atmosphere at this bland air-conditioned restaurant, but the tasty Chinese fare is some of the best you will find outside Colombo, albeit spiced up for local palates with stray bits of chilli and lemongrass.

Rams $ *11 D.S. Senanayake Road.* Rams offers excellent South Indian vegetarian fare – *dosas, vadais, thalis* and *lassis* galore – at bargain prices. The dishes are served up in an endearingly kitsch setting complete with lots of wooden parrots and murals of sari-clad maidens.

THE HILL COUNTRY

The Hill Club $$ *Off Grand Hotel Road, tel: 052-222 2653.* If you have ever wondered what colonial life in Sri Lanka was like, a visit to this venerable hotel is a good way to find out. The food itself is pretty average, but the real attraction is the time-warped colonial aura of the evening meal, which is served promptly at 8pm by white-gloved waiters in the chintzy dining room. It's all strangely compelling and oddly romantic. Ladies really *do* dress for dinner here, while men are only admitted if clad in the obligatory jacket and tie (though these are available free at the club if you don't have your own).

King Prawn $$ *Glendower Hotel, Grand Hotel Road, tel: 052-222 2501.* The food at this cosy little restaurant is about as authentic as Chinese cooking gets in Sri Lanka, although still with enough spice to keep the hill-country chills at bay.

St Andrew's Hotel $$$ *10 St Andrew's Drive, tel: 052-222 3031.* The atmospheric oak-panelled restaurant at Nuwara Eliya's smartest hotel offers a homely setting for old-fashioned European-colonial-style cooking, with lots of hearty meat dishes and one of the island's biggest wine lists.

THE EAST

Siam View Hotel $ *Arugam Bay, tel: 063-224 8195.* This popular guesthouse is home to a wooden Thai-style restaurant complete with genuine resident Thai chef who prepares a range of spicy curries and other southeast Asian dishes. This restaurant is a surprising but very welcome feature of the remote east-coast surfers' village of Arugam Bay.

INDEX